Flyleaf Journal
Volume One
2014

Copyright © 2014 by *Flyleaf*

EDITOR: Matthew Jankiewicz
ASSISTANT EDITORS: Parker Stockman
                              Chasity Deal
ART DIRECTION AND DESIGN: Skinner
LOGO DESIGN: Marcus Deely

Published by:
Flyleaf Inc.
6627 Old Oaks Blvd.
Pearland, TX 77584

Permissions appear at the end of the book.

ISBN: 978-1502556813

Printed in the United States of America

Visit us on the web at www.FlyleafJournal.com

FLYLEAF

Contents

Flyleaf Journal
Volume One
2014

Eric Charles May
The Girl Who Wished

Once upon a time, way back in the 1950s, when there was no cyber or cable anything and the cars were all big and boxy, there was a little girl who lived with her mother and father, just the three of them, in a fine brick house on the Far South Side of Chicago. (Only Negro people, as they called themselves back then, lived in the neighborhood, nearly all of them also living in fine brick houses.) The Girl's favorite part of the day was evening when her Daddy returned from work. No matter the season, she'd wait on the front steps, anxious for the sight of his tall, dark figure walking down the street. If he was whistling, The Girl knew he was happy and she'd run to him so he could grab her with his large hands and lift her up.

"Hey there Caramel," he'd say. (He called her "Caramel" because he said that's what her color reminded him of, which made The Girl happy because it was her Mommy's color too.)

Her Daddy's face was scratchy and smelled like burning leaves. After a hug and kiss, he would carry her inside. However, if he wasn't whistling as he approached, then The Girl knew he was sad. On such evenings she waited on the steps and he passed her without saying a word and she knew she must not make noise that evening because Daddy might get mad and yell at her.

Her mother and father yelled at each other a lot, especially at night after The Girl went to bed. She'd hide under the covers but could still hear them. It made her cry to hear the angry voices, so one night she prayed to God.

"I wish Mommy and Daddy wouldn't fight anymore," she said.

"Alright, you'll have your wish," she heard God say.

The next Sunday when she and her mother returned home from church, her father was gone, along with all his clothes. She never saw him again.

The Girl's playmates (who were all Negroes too) soon took to teasing her. They'd heard their parents talking of how The Girl's father had run off with someone named Wanda Williams.

"Where your daddy girl?" the kids teased.

"In his skin!" The Girl answered defiantly.

And when she walked away, they sang behind her:

> "*Someone's in the kitchen with Wan-da.*
> *Someone's in the kitchen I know-oh-oh-oh.*
> *Mister Foster in the kitchen with Wan-daaa,*
> *And she's playing on his banjo!*"

A few months later, The Girl and her Mommy left the fine brick house and moved into a small apartment set above a neighborhood storefront because they didn't have any money. The Girl was mad at God. Her wish had been for Mommy and Daddy to stop fighting, not for Daddy to leave. The Girl swore she'd never talk to God again.

* * *

The years passed and passed all the way to the 1970s when folks wore long hair and bell-bottoms. By then, The Girl had grown tall and cover-girl shapely and attended community college, which is where she finally made her first real best friend. The friend's name was Sheila. She had dark skin and a wide smile that made you feel she had some sneaky fun in mind. Sheila and The Girl were very different. Whereas The Girl wanted everything five minutes ago, Sheila was patient as a tree; The Girl was an authority on fancy clothes, Sheila had no fashion sense whatsoever; The Girl cared nothing for current events while Sheila read newspapers galore.

Despite all this, The Girl and Sheila loved each other's company. They had fun doing everything and nothing. They gave each other advice. They finished each other's sentences. In conversation, each knew when to ask a question and when to just listen.

Then, after junior year, Sheila moved to New York City— alone. In letters home Sheila wrote that Manhattan was simply, "too wonderful." It made The Girl sad (not to mention a little angry) that her friend was having such a good time without her.

One night, The Girl sat in her bedroom at home drinking a beer she'd snuck in past her mother. While gazing at the photograph of Sheila smiling in Central Park, she became so unhappy she broke her promise and prayed to God again. "I wish Sheila was home."

"Alright, if that's what you want," she was sure she heard God say.

A month later, Sheila returned home. Sheila was sick. Doctors gave her lots of treatments, but none did any good.

After Sheila died The Girl was really mad at God. She vowed she'd never, ever, talk to him again. He might be the Almighty, but she also knew he couldn't be trusted.

Not long after that, The Girl left college and got a boring secretary job. She dated lots of men to ease the tedium but they were boring too, even the ones she slept with.

One night, when she was awfully drunk and angry after reading Sheila's old letters, The Girl decided to pray to The Devil.

"I want a handsome man to marry who has lots of money. And let my baby be a boy because life's easier on them than it is on girls."

"I think that can be arranged," she heard The Devil say.

She laughed and didn't give it another thought. But a year later at a picnic she met a Handsome Man. He was so un-brown that when her mother first met him, she thought he was a White man. His family was rich and he was engaged to a woman as un-brown as he. But after the picnic he said he wanted to marry The Girl instead. The Girl didn't love the Handsome Man like the women do in romantic movies, but as her mother told her: "Child, life is not the movies."

The Girl said yes to the Handsome Man's proposal, which didn't please his mother. "She's not Catholic," his mother protested. "She's too dark and she's stupid." But The Girl converted and married the Handsome Man anyway. They moved into a big house way up on the North Side in Lincoln Park where hardly any Black people (as they now called themselves) resided.

At first The Girl was happy being married, then after a while she wasn't; so she gave in to the wishes of her husband and agreed to have a baby. Soon she was pregnant, but after six months, for some reason, her body pushed the baby out, the poor child breathless. She later learned from Her Husband The Handsome Man (who insisted on learning every detail of every little thing) that the baby had been female.

A year later The Girl was pregnant again. This time everything was fine until nearly the eighth month when, again, her body pushed the baby out before it was ready. After living for an hour, this child died too.

With tearful eyes Her Husband The Handsome Man said they must name this baby (which The Girl thought of as Dead Baby Number 2). The Girl said naming was morbid but Her Husband the Handsome Man insisted. The child must be named for the sake of its immortal soul, he said, which is how Joan Frances Woodbury came to be buried in the Woodbury family plot.

Convinced the Devil had killed her first two children because neither was the boy she'd wished for, The Girl was all guilt and loathing when she got home from the hospital. Unfortunately, Her Husband the Handsome Man had been so sad during her stay that he forgot about the nursery, which she found still intact.

The Girl became furious. She opened the nursery's second story window and flung away the cotton diapers and stuffed animals and baby jammies; the items landing in the front yard.

People walking down the quiet street stopped to look. (It was late on a Saturday morning, very cold but with no snow.) Out the window sailed plastic bottles of baby oil, baby powder, baby formula, then a folded blue pram in mint condition, then a white bassinet, and then glass baby bottles that shattered on the walkway. The flying shards forced the half-dozen gawkers to step back from the low, front gate. They all thought the Black woman up there must be crazy. (The onlookers were all White people.) Then just like that the Black woman disappeared from the window and they heard yelling coming from inside the house. As it turned out, Her Husband the Handsome Man had been in his first floor den with his rosary, praying for poor Joan Frances. It wasn't till he heard bottles breaking that he rushed to the living room picture window. He then took the stairs two at a time to the second floor, arriving at the top as The Girl was pushing the rolling crib into the hallway.

"Things aren't bad enough," she yelled, "I have to come home to this?"

Gripping the crib's headboard she shoved it into him and knocked him to the floor, then she pushed the bed over the top stair and sent the thing crashing all the way to the landing, after which she turned to Her Husband The Handsome Man, who was rising from the floor, and growled: "There-is-no-baby-in-this-house, understand?"

She stomped down the stairs, stepping around the toppled crib at the bottom. Grabbing her black wool coat from the foyer closet, she opened the front door onto the trashed yard. The onlookers by then had been joined by two White men police officers, their car parked in the middle of the street with blue lights flashing.

Her eyes large with rage, her hair sticking wildly from her head (for she had not been to the hairdresser's for some time), the cops asked her what was wrong.

"Wrong?" she sneered while pulling on the coat. "Why, every-thing's just fine!"

She made a move to go and one of the officers raised a hand to stop her.

The Girl pointed her finger at him.

"This is my yard. This is my stuff. If I want to throw stuff out my window it's my business."

The officer's face went red. He was about to speak when his partner motioned to the still open doorway where Her Husband the Handsome Man was now standing.

"It's okay," he said to the cops. "Let her go. She lives here."

The cops stepped aside and The Girl stormed past, yelling at a few of the onlookers to get the hell out of her way. They all watched as she headed down the block, hands jammed in her coat pockets, shoulders hunched against the cold.

The Girl didn't return home till after dark. The porch light was on and the yard cleared, save for the bits of glass: teensy glimmers under the whitish glare.

A few years later The Girl got pregnant yet again—prophylactic malfunction—and this time there was no baby shower or talk of names or heart-to-hearts with her mom about mothering.

The baby was born a healthy boy. Her Husband the Handsome Man asked what was her choice for a name. Gazing with disinterest at the hospital TV she said, "Call him whatever you want." So, he named the un-dead baby Charles Breton Woodbury—Brett for short. He was so pretty, even The Girl's snarky Mother-In-Law couldn't look at the kid without smiling. But The Girl was not fooled. She knew God and The Devil were just waiting for her to weaken and fall madly in love with her son so she'd start wishing good things for him, which God and The Devil would then use as a means to destroy the boy, just like they'd destroyed her parents' marriage, and Sheila, and her daughters. The Girl gave Brett a respectable amount of attention, but not so much that she'd succumb to any desires to adore him. She kept her emotions in check, she watched her step, and she never wished for anything again.

Christina Murphy

Accidental Falls

My mother, returning with a bottle of wine borrowed from a neighbor for the party at which people drank more than she expected, tripped over a piece of broken pavement, fell onto the sidewalk, and took a chunk of skin off her palms. The bottle shattered. My mother, a hysteric by nature, screamed and cried and drew a crowd—my father chief among them, who discovered that a shard of the green bottle glass had imbedded itself in the center of my mother's forehead. He removed it gingerly, telling her it was all right, she was not hurt. This was no comfort to my mother, who was fixated on that she could have been blinded. This was my mother's world, the could-have-been of multiple horrors and outcomes. He helped her to her feet. She was still crying as the crowd gathered round, giving her comfort with the one platitude she claimed as her own—how awful that this should happen to her.

I was on our front steps, watching, a ten year-old aware of my mother's high-strung nature, my father's inability to be enough to keep her calm, and my own sense of curiosity as to whether the glass shard would leave a scar on my mother's beautiful forehead and thus make my father's life and mine an endless nightmare of the horrible things that one could never get over in life, because, after all, the wounds were there forever, were they not?

And she was right about that. My father did not succeed in removing all the glass, and a sliver buried deep in her forehead soon festered and swelled into a marble-sized knot that required the expertise of a doctor to excise. Five stitches and a two-week dose of antibiotics, and soon the swelling disappeared and the wound healed, but left in its wake a noticeable indentation and a small white scar.

For my mother, this was devastating—a deep tragedy. It was the loss of her beauty, which was no longer perfect but marred. When she looked in the mirror, the scar was all she saw. And she was convinced that it was all anyone else saw, too. Not her high cheekbones, her full lips, or her autumn brown eyes. Not the striking tone and glow of her olive skin with its burnished softness. Not any of it. Just the indentation and the scar.

There was no consoling my mother. There was no comfort, no hope, in telling her it was a tiny imperfection, barely noticeable. To my mother, it became the world.

And gradually, in her anguish over her loss of perfection, my father and I drifted from her sight and from her world. We were no help in assuaging her sadness,. Instead, we served only as reminders of the past. Soon we became symbols of everything she resented for ruining her life.

And so it went on like this—she moving farther away, and my father and I drawing closer together. In time, I became immersed in my own world of dreams and fantasies, and my father sought release in his job as an accountant. He found in his columns of numbers and graphs a new love that filled his soul and countered my mother's disdain.

What my mother did with her days was unknown to us. Sometimes she was home, but mostly she was gone. In her absence, my father and I ate meals together—breakfasts at fast food places that created fluffy yellow scrambled eggs from egg substitutes, lunches of sandwich meats on grocery store bread made soft and pliant by added chemicals, and pot pies for our dinners. We did not talk much during these meals and never mentioned my mother. She came and went very much like a moth drawn to the light in the darkness and withdrawing in silence during the daylight.

It was not until years had gone by that we learned she had spent many of her days with a friend of my father's, who lived only two streets away. He read to her during the days and evenings. This part, my father and I had the hardest time understanding. We expected an affair, perhaps even a friendship. but the sharing of books made no sense to either of us.

My mother had never expressed any interest in reading. Her focus was on fashion; clothing and jewelry had always been her passion. And travel—she would have gone anywhere around the world given the chance and perhaps never come back if finances permitted. But books and ideas, were not, as she might say, her cup of tea.

It was the letters that affected my father and me the most. My father's friend had the tenderness to touch my mother's small, delicate scar—even to kiss it sweetly in those moments when she was most sad at the loss of her fine beauty that had brought her so much pleasure and constant male attention in life. Apparently, he understood something my father and I did not—the longing for the touch, the kiss, that made my mother feel whole once more and desirable. We had only words to offer, and words were not enough.

My father's friend would sit next to my mother on the couch, put his arm around her to draw her near, and read to her. Poetry was her favorite. Poems were short, and after each poem, she would receive a gentle, delicate kiss on her forehead, the man's lips finding ways to say everything my father and I could not. The tenderness was touching, and it made my father feel empty. Eventually it made my father feel bitter, and soon he was as consumed with his bitterness as my mother was with her scar. I was in the middle and lost. There was no room for me inside his bitterness or her sense of how tragically life had treated her. The times I was home, I was mostly alone. I ate potpies by myself and wondered where my father went in the days and evenings that my mother was with my father's friend. It became unimportant for me to be at home because nothing I had to offer mattered. My words were ineffective, just as my offers to listen were dismissed as irrelevant.

From his diary and a handful of notes I found after my father's death, I learned that he had gone to listen to music in those times he no longer wished to be home. Jazz—the coolness, the unpredictability, the freedom, and the wonder. It had all captivated him and lifted his spirits beyond the heavy weight of my mother's isolation. He no longer needed her and did not care that she no longer needed him.

I would like to believe that the high call of a trumpet or the low wail of a saxophone against the wild or gentle rhythms of a piano set my father's world right. Nothing I could say ever did. His loss was too extreme. But I am at peace with that, knowing that I did what I could, even if I did not understand all that was expected, but not really needed, from me. Each of us, in our own way, failed ourselves and failed each other. Or so my father's last entry in his diary said, and I believe him.

Sahar Mustafah
Torn

We sat cross-legged on my bed, the globe wobbling between us on its plastic stand, and you turned it until a part of Asia and all of Australia faced me. You pressed your palm against Africa and teased a corner of South America until you peeled it off, taking most of the Atlantic Ocean with you. I held my breath, worried you were going to tear it away from the rest of the world— much too easily—and ball it up and throw it into my wastebasket.

But you let it hang there, and when I slowly spun the world I pushed my fingers through the hole as though, at nine years old, I might feel water and seaweed and a shoal of fish and maybe the rough dorsal ridges of a whale.

You were ten then, older and wiser, and said if I could actually reach in and touch the core of the earth my entire hand would instantly melt from red-hot magma. I pulled out my fingers and carefully lifted the thin paper and pressed it into its proper place, but it wouldn't stick.

Now you, twenty years old, stare at the globe on the wooden

It's because of your mom, isn't it? you say, and I hear something catch in your voice like the time we were kids and you couldn't save Smokey after a pick-up ran him down. We were playing tag when we heard a horrible yelp. You wouldn't let the driver—a man wearing a corduroy jacket and the sorriest look I'd ever seen on a grownup—help you carry Smokey into the house. The fur along his neck was matted down with blood so Smokey looked wet like he'd been running and barking in the rain as he loved to do. But he was dead and limp and you held him and wouldn't let go until your dad unfurled your arms from around Smokey's body and gently carried him and laid him in the flat bed of his truck.

"Yes," I tell you, "it's because of my mom."

I tuck strands of outgrown bangs behind my ears, bangs I cut myself with my mother's sewing scissors the summer before our senior year. When we weren't together, I'd spend time leafing through *Vogue* and wanted so desperately to be like Kate Moss and those other runway models. They were the kind of girls you didn't like, but I still wanted to be beautiful and stylish, and I figured if I cut my hair I'd get a little closer.

My mother came home that day and found me in the bathroom, wisps of hair shorn like grass from a blade. They had fallen obliviously into the sink. I had cut my hair with a vengeful hope.

She told me there were no more treatments left, that she had exhausted every possibility. Her face was so pale that the circles under her eyes grew darker as the days passed. *I just want to be home with my family*, she said. She used that word—family—though it was only the two of us, and Nana, who secretly called my father in Denver, but he never returned her messages.

That day she came home from the clinic, she stared down at the fragments of my hair—dark chestnut color like hers before bureau. My mother's orchid plant sits in a ceramic bowl beside it, flowers newly opened. One of its branches almost touches the ceiling of my room.

We sit on my bed—you on the edge, naked and lean, your shoulders broad and taut from years of swim practice. Your mother used to drop you off at Elsner High School in her cotton nightdress, a grey wool coat and winter boots before the sun broke through the great pines of Bowling Ridge where we used to sit in that abandoned car, holding hands and not kissing, though I wanted to.

She wore the same coat to my mother's funeral a year ago and never took it off, even afterwards when she helped my aunts serve casserole and beer. She only unbuttoned it so she could stretch out her arms to pull paper plates off a high shelf in the pantry. When she hugged me close, her sleeves chafed against my cheek and she smelled faintly of lemon dish soap.

On my bed your back is to me now, and I watch the ripples of muscles as you breathe. I tie my mother's robe tightly around my waist, waiting for you to turn around and look at me, but you won't.

Outside my window fallen maple leaves rustle and blow across the backyard. Dawn breaks and a goldfinch twitters on a roof shingle, then is silent. I listen for another moment and wonder if it has flown away. It rained all night and you pulled off your work boots, their soles covered in patches of brown and damp grass, before entering the kitchen.

As sunlight gathers in my room, you tell me I won't survive the desert, that girls like me didn't fight ragheads. I scoot closer to you and the mattress creaks.

"I won't be fighting," I tell you, "I'll be a medic and you won't change my mind." I trace the wing-bone in your shoulder.

clumps of it had begun to fall on the cool floor tiles of the stall when she showered. She pressed one hand against the glass door and crouched down to vomit into the drain. I'd sit on the toilet seat and watch the water stream down her face, mingling with her tears until I could no longer tell the difference. I'd patiently wait, clutching her white robe in my lap, getting ready to wrap her in it as soon as she stepped onto the sea-green bath rug.

I hear the goldfinch twitter again, closer, on my windowsill. Your back's still to me as you say, *You'll regret it. It's not what you think it is over there.*

"How would you know?" I respond, and then you dip your shoulder away from my touch and finally turn to face me.

I don't know, you mumble.

The only hair on your chest gathers like sleek feathers in the hollow space between your pecs. I press two fingertips into your strawberry blond tuft. You never shaved it for swim meets and the other boys had teased you about it being the difference of a millisecond on your recorded time.

"I'm going," I say again, but this time it's a whisper while I look straight into your speckled blue eyes. They are lightest when you are naked, when they don't absorb the color of your favorite denim shirt, which lays wrinkled on the floor after I had gently pulled it off your shoulders last night. It's still damp from the rain.

Ten weeks later, you won't come to my graduation from basic training because you'd been drinking the night before at Fatty's Pub and you pass out in your brother's car at the mouth of Bowling Ridge. A morning jogger sees you and calls the state police. You miss the Amtrak to Georgia.

I'll be transferred to Fort Sam Houston for my MOS and a year later, you'll drive nearly two thousand miles to see me in a car you rented with money from your new job at your uncle's insurance agency. When you're a motel away, I'll text you that maybe it's not a good idea for you to visit after all. I don't tell you it's been lonelier than I could've ever imagined and I've been sleeping with another recruit who doesn't look at me when he's thrusting inside. But you've known it all along. I can still feel the flutter of your eyelashes against my temples when we rocked against each other's body.

You show up anyway, wearing dark-wash jeans and a disheveled sports coat I don't recognize. "Fancy," I say. You look smaller. Your shoulders seem to have shrunk beneath the weight of fabric and I wonder if your wingspan is still magnificent and fierce.

I stand before you, erect in fatigue pants and a desert-colored t-shirt. My hair's in a tight ponytail, no longer deep-conditioned or smelling like strawberries—just clean. I hope you won't tell me how proud my mother would have been.

Instead you smile and take my hand across the table at the Denny's and say, *I never did know how to let go.*

Neither have I.

Cynthia Scott

A Sense of Humor

She rubbed her eyes twice when she saw the hand. It lay between the rows of collard greens, gray and waxen, cut clean at the wrist, with dull fingernails, clenched fingers, and clotted blood around the clean, white bone. It looked like something for sale at a Halloween store, something trickster children might use to scare the bejeezus out of little old ladies, except that it wasn't made of rubber. Flies buzzed around it and black ants trooped over it, tearing its flesh with their powerful mandibles and carrying away the bits to God knew where.

Vernice reeled back and threw up in the dirt.

She ran into the house and called her husband, Mel, who told her to sit tight; he was coming right over. She did as he told her. Literally. She sat in the living room and didn't move a muscle. When Mel arrived, wearing his sanitation department jumpsuit and a SF Giants cap pulled down over his eyes, he asked her where it was. He did not acknowledge what "it" was. She pointed meekly toward the backyard patio door. It was still open, drawing in cold air.

"Where it at, Vern?" he asked again.

Vernice told him, her mouth still tasting of vomit. Mel went outside. He returned a few moments later, his face ashen. It seemed to Vern that he had acquired a few more gray hairs in his beard, a few more lines around his eyes.

"We gotta call the cops," she said.

He creased his brow and bit down on the corner of his lip. She expected him to say, 'hell no.' He hated cops, had been pulled over by them too many times to count and for no reason at all. When he was nineteen he had been roughed up by them and tossed in jail, the victim of mistaken identity. He would have been railroaded to prison (the cops were that convinced they had their guy, and who was going to tell them otherwise?) had it not been for the fact that the person who had done the deed turned himself in. So she didn't expect Mel to want anything to do with cops, even for a reason like this, but he surprised her.

"Do it," he said. "Call 'em. Goddammit."

First came the uniforms. Then forensics. They trampled through the house, trampled through her kitchen garden, writing things down on notepads, marking spots in her garden, bagging items, canvassing the alleyway behind their backyard, taking photographs. She had never seen so many cops in her life. Mel kept out of their way. After answering their questions, he went back to work; he couldn't afford to take a day off. He didn't want to be around because of the cops and the hand that still lay in the garden like a tuberous root springing from the ground. It was too much for him. He preferred the steadiness and simplicity of collecting garbage.

Vern stayed in the house. She sat on the couch and watched TV. She was staring at the screen while the uniformed cops questioned her. They asked her to tell her story. She told them how she woke up that morning with an odd feeling that something bad was going to happen, though she did not know what. She went downstairs and made breakfast for Mel before he went to work. She described the breakfast—eggs and bacon; toast and coffee. She mentioned how she had burned the toast because she was so distracted by this lingering omen until one of the cops told her to tell them how she found the hand. But that was the point she was leading up to, the point of the story she was foreshadowing. She wanted to build toward that, not for their sake, but for her own. She wanted to prepare herself when she revisited that awful moment when she discovered the hand in her garden, the moment when she realized it was real, that this awful thing lying in her beautiful garden had once belonged to another human being.

When she told the story a second time to the detectives who arrived shortly after, she embellished, lingered over the feeling in her stomach, the burned toast, the awful sensation when she realized the hand was real. She relived the moment again in her mind, shaping it so that she had control over it, control over her own reaction to it. The detectives let her speak. They nodded politely, jotted what she said down onto their notepads, asked questions: did she notice any strange activities the night before? Can she recall any strange noises, anything that seemed unusual? But she kept lingering at that moment when she realized the hand was real.

She repeated the story to her neighbors who gathered outside, watching the street and foot traffic in their small, quiet neighborhood. She told them that awful feeling she had, the omen, and they nodded and understood. Hadn't the same thing happened to Beverly Raymond when she found out her son had been killed? That whole day before the cops came knocking on her door she had had a terrible feeling, like something was crushing down inside her. She knew something terrible had happened. She called her son, and when she could not reach him she called his girlfriend and his friends, and when they did not give her answers she got an even deeper, more awful feeling inside.

"When they knocked on her door," said one of the neighbors, "she just knew Clayton was gone."

"Um, hm," said another. "You always know."

Vernice nodded because she understood now too, how knowing and feeling and understanding were all one in the same. So, by the time she was interviewed by the local television stations, she led with that simple truth: "I had a bad feeling something was wrong."

Later that day, after the police finally departed, leaving behind the yellow tape they had wound around her backyard fence, the muddy footprints on her carpet, and the general air of disturbance, she locked all the doors and windows and waited for Mel to come home. Too unsettled to start dinner, she watched TV instead, recording the segments reported on the local news of "the incident." She learned that the police were waiting for more forensic evidence to determine whether to investigate this as a homicide. They continued to canvas neighborhoods, asking more questions. The news anchors all led with the story about "a bizarre incident in Richmond," and broadcast her interview. On each channel, it began differently--"I had a bad feeling" to "I knew something was wrong" to "Just had a feeling, something weren't right." In each variation the story was still the same, but compressed—polished.

Her friend Avie called and said, "Turn to CNN. They got

you on there too." Her daughter Noreen called from Atlanta and said she "had gone viral." A clip of her interview was posted on YouTube, which she thought was strange, but on the whole everything that entire day had been strange.

"Looks like you're famous now, Mama," Rennie said.

But fame seemed beside the point.

After Mel returned home, they exchanged stories. Word had gotten round to the department about what happened, so Mel's coworkers bombarded him with questions, explanations, requests for details. He told them as best he could, but he always lingered over that unsettled feeling he had of having so many damn cops in his home. He retold the times he had been roughed up, beaten up, thrown in jail, accused of crimes he hadn't committed, and so couldn't wait to get the hell out of his own home. His own damn home! They nodded, understanding, but he repeated it to them: "That's my damn home and they all up in there, asking me where I been at and what I been doing, acting like I had something to do with that goddamned hand." Vern rubbed his shoulder as he recounted his story and she nodded and understood and retold her own story again, although this time the more polished version, the version she told to the media, and not the first version she told him when he came home earlier that morning, still raw and brutal in its visceral experience.

"I just had a feeling something bad had happened," she said. "That's why I ended up burning that toast."

Mel nodded and rubbed his chin. "Whoever did it, though, knew what they was doing, 'cause I didn't hear nothing last night."

"Me neither."

"It was quiet as church last night, wasn't it? Didn't hear nobody running around in that alleyway back there. And you know how the Barkers' dog be howling anytime somebody walking through there. Didn't hear a peep."

"That's what I told the police. I didn't hear nothing strange last night."

"They must've sneaked through there quiet as mice and tossed it over our fence."

He shook his head. Vernice rubbed his shoulder.

"They were slick about it though: you gotta hand that to 'em."

They paused for a moment, both realizing what he had said, and started laughing.

"They must've had a helping hand," he said and they broke into another volley of laughter. Mel was on a roll. "Hands down, they knew exactly what they were doing."

"Now, Mel," she said, slapping his back. "Come on now."

"They didn't want no hand in any of it."

"Oh, Good Lord," Vern said, sputtering with laughter. "My poor collard greens, too."

"Just so you know, I ain't eating none of them collard greens now. We could be living hand to mouth, and I still wouldn't eat that shit."

"Mel," she cried. "Stop it. Stop it now. You ain't right."

But he continued with his jokes and Vern continued laughing and thanking God she married a man who still had a good sense of humor.

Patricia Ann McNair
Good News or Money

*H*ello, *is this someone with good news or money? No? Goodbye!*

Er…

Hello, is this someone with good news or money? No? Goodbye!

Ha! Yeah, right. *A Thousand Clowns*. Jason Robards. Right. Ok, yeah. Hey. It's me. Surprise. Long time. I know.

So here's the thing. It's about Mom. Are you there? Are you listening? Can you hear me? It's about Mom, she asked me to call. I didn't want to, but she asked…

Hello, is this someone with good news or money? No? Goodbye!

Goddamn machine. You wait a minute to try to collect your thoughts. It's about Mom, right? I got something to say.

Oh, wait. You probably think I'm calling about something

bad. Oh, jeez. Wow. That's not…I mean…it's not bad. Nothing bad. No, hey. It's good. Ok, take two. Or whatever.

Hi, Dad? It's me. You know. Your daughter? The one you haven't seen in what, six years? Not since you moved up north—to the tundra or whatever? Well, the only one, I guess. Your only daughter. Maybe. As far as I know. Probably. Your only daughter, probably. Does that sound harsh? Sorry.

It's just…I've been thinking about things, you know? Things. Just things. All kinds of things…

Hello, is this someone with good news or money? No? Goodbye!

Goddamnit! Are you sure you aren't there?

You always loved that movie, *A Thousand Clowns*. I remember. You made me watch it with you, what, a hundred times? Jason fucking Robards. That little kid who looked like a miniature man. Anyway. Mom wanted me to call you. She's got some news. So yeah, good news, I guess. Good news. But no money. Ha! That's a laugh, *me* telling *you* no money. When was the last time you sent us any money, Dad? Daddy-o? Remember when I used to call you that? I was little. Really little. Daddy's little girl you used to call me.

I'm seventeen now. But you know that. You should. You do, don't you? I'm seventeen.

Aw, shit. Hang on. I gotta blow my nose.

Hello, is this someone with good news or money? No? Goodbye!

I keep expecting you're gonna pick up the phone one of these times. Maybe you do. Maybe you do pick up the phone. Funny, but when I remember your voice, it sounds like Jason Robards in that movie. Sorta smoked rough. Is that you, Dad? Are you on the line?

So here's the thing, Dad. Daddy-o. I have been thinking about that one time for some reason. Remember? That time you came home without your shoes and said you'd given them to some guy on the street. Some guy who needed them more than you, some homeless guy who lived on the street you said (what street was that exactly, Dad? Daddy-o. I always wondered what street was that exactly.)

I'm a little off topic here. Mom asked me to call. That's why I'm calling. She asked me to. To tell you the news.

But that time you came home without your shoes, Dad. I can't stop thinking about it. There you were, in socks on the icy tile floor of the foyer, and you said you gave this guy your shoes because it was cold and he was barefoot. It was early morning. Spring. I remember the sky was sort of purple, it was so early. Purple like a bruise. Like grape jelly.

You remember. You must. We were in that yellow house in New Hope. The one with the tile floors and the toilet that always overflowed. The one with the basement that flooded all the time and smelled like wet dog. The one where Mom was pregnant for a little while.

And then she wasn't.

You remember.

And we didn't know where you'd been, me and Mom, and then there you were, wiggling your keys in the door like you didn't know which one worked and then you were inside and we were watching TV, me and Mom, the morning news, just in case. Just in case you were on it. In case you were news. An accident or something. Hurt maybe. But you didn't look hurt. Just shoeless.

And Mom was eating dry toast to try to keep from puking, the morning sickness was bad. And I was eating Lucky Charms.

The yellow house. You remember…

* * *

Hello, is this someone with good news or money? No? Goodbye!

Goddamnit! That was my fault that time. I hit the wrong button.

So Mom's news. Yeah. But wait, the yellow house first.

You went to bed without telling us where you were all night, but we could tell you'd been drinking (not like we didn't know that already, but we could tell.) And Mom seemed okay that you had given your shoes away, happy even. Because it was something good you'd been up to. She was like that for a long time, you remember. Always wanting things to be good, to be right. Even that time we got evicted and they threw all of our stuff out on the lawn, she was out there making neat piles in front of the yellow house, loading what she could into the taxi, but making sure the rest was all orderly. Right. It was better that way, she told me. Maybe. Whatever.

But then a little later—I'm back to the morning you came home without your shoes. Sorry. Jumping around a bit here. Anyway, later that day without your shoes, when the sun was high and hot, and the kids were playing out in the backyards and someone was mowing the lawn somewhere—I always loved that smell of cut grass, so I didn't even mind when you made me do the mowing—this lady sneaks up our walk and takes something out from a shopping bag and she's looking nervous. And something else. Drunk, maybe. We're watching her out the picture window, me and Mom, we could see her from where we were on the couch. Do you remember that couch? You bought it on time. I came home one day from school, and it wasn't there anymore. Just a place on the rug that looked cleaner than the rest of the floor.

So this woman is on the front step and Mom pulls open the door, and the lady is there stuffing something—notebook paper or something—into your shoes. Pushing the toes right up against the screen door, neat, like she's setting them out for you or something. And Mom says, "hey!" –that's all she says: "hey!" The lady's eyes are sore-looking and blue and she smiles, says "excuse me," says, "his shoes." And I'm over Mom's shoulder and the woman sees me and smiles again, but the smile breaks. Like it was plastic. Jeez, I don't even know what that means, but I thought that then. I remember it now. Her smile broke like something plastic. And she turns and runs away...

Hello, is this someone with good news or money? No? Goodbye!

Ok. This isn't why I called. This trip down memory lane or whatever. I called because Mom asked me to. She wanted you to know. She's getting married. She's happy. She wanted you to know.

But now I got something to say. I only now thought of it. And it's about your favorite movie. *A Thousand Clowns.* Jason Robards is a bad father. He's an asshole. In the movie, I mean. I never liked that movie. It made my stomach hurt.

Because I can't help remembering the one time you sat there in the living room on a kitchen chair where the couch used to be with a beer beside you on the floor. And the damn tape of that movie is on and you are staring at it like it's something important, maybe. Like there is something you have to learn from it.

"Dad," I said. "Daddy-o." Remember?

And you didn't even look at me.

"Mom's sick, Dad." And she was. She'd been bleeding since morning, only I didn't know that right then. I was too little to know much, but I knew enough. I knew she was curled up in a ball on the bed, and there was a towel underneath her and another one soaking pink in the bathtub. And she was sweating and crying.

"She's sick, Dad."

And you turned to me finally, and your eyes were big black holes. You blinked. And your face was wet. And you nodded. You got up then, and went into the kitchen. And I could hear you in there on the phone. And then you came back with a fresh beer and sat on the kitchen chair and rewound the damn movie to where it was before you got up.

And in a few minutes, I could hear a siren.

So. There's that.

Anyway.

Mom told me to call you. She told me to tell you she forgives you now, but I told her I wouldn't tell you that. Because really, who can forgive a father for loving a movie more than his own wife, his own daughter. Because I think that sums it up pretty goddamn accurately.

And besides that, who can forgive a father for coming home without his shoes?

Not me. No sir. Not me.

Ok, then. That's all I got. No good news, not really. And no money. Just this. That's all. Ok.

Denton Loving

Into the Darkest Heart

How the Father Loved

My father had a son. The son was me. My father's own father had died the year before, and the birth of the child partially filled that hole. The child's arrival was a relief. It was a spring day after a long winter. It was hope realized. The son was hope. I was the son, and I was hope fulfilled.

My father had a son that he didn't know what to do with. So he carried his son with him everywhere he went.

My father had a son, and he became a stay at home dad. He didn't consider himself a pioneer in gender equality. He didn't see himself riding the front of the wave of stay at home fathers. He didn't think about gender roles at all.

My father had a son, who was more than he bargained for, as all children are. He knew children must be watched vigilantly, but even the quietest child—perhaps especially the quietest child—will escape from vigilance, only to be found playing in the toilet or hidden in a cabinet or gone altogether with only the front door left ajar.

My father had a son, and once, when the father fell deeply into the exhausted sleep of stay at home fathers, the son escaped the house in silence and walked through the playground and two blocks down the sidewalk to a busy intersection. The child was practicing, even at this early age, to always find the easiest escape. He saw the golden arches of a McDonald's another block away before he decided to turn back.

My father had a son, and when the son grew old enough to want to prove his independence, the son told a story about walking unsupervised to McDonald's when he was three years old, but the father assured him it wasn't true.

My father had a son who went everywhere with his father: to garages and barber shops and grocery stores and feed mills and banks and other places where old men sat and loafed like it was Sunday afternoon, even though it wasn't.

My father had a son who didn't want to go with him. The son was tired of standing around, always being told not to touch, impatiently waiting in garages and barber shops and grocery stores and feed mills and banks and other places where old men sat and loafed like it was Sunday afternoon, which it never was.

My father had a son who wanted to stay home. The son was bookish and introverted, and when the father wanted to leave the house, he had to make the son go along, and there were tears and much fighting and general exasperation.

My father had a son who was bookish and introverted, and when the father wanted to leave the house, he left the son alone, because, he reasoned, the boy was old enough, and responsible, and it was what he wanted, and frankly it was what the father wanted too.

My father had a son who stayed at home by himself when other people thought he was too young.

My father had a son who stayed at home by himself when other people thought he was just the right age.

My father had a son who stayed at home by himself and only opened the door for people he knew.

My father had a son who stayed at home by himself, and although he was told not to, he opened his door to anyone and everyone.

How the Mother Loved

My mother had a son. The son was me. Her clock had been ticking in overtime, and the healthy birth of the child seemed even more momentous because of how long she had waited. The child's arrival was a relief. It was the bloom of a rose long after the bush has been planted. It was the answer to the prayer. The son was the answer. I was the son, and I was the answer to my mother's prayer.

My mother had a son that she left with her husband to raise while she went back to work. She was happiest at work, where she taught other people's children. After school, the children returned to their own parents, and she returned to her own child.

My mother had a son that she left, anguished each morning by his cries not to go to school, not to leave him. Every day, her heart broke a little more, but she left. And every evening, when other people's children had exhausted her, her own son greeted her unhappily, taking almost an hour every day to forget how she had left and why he must punish her.

My mother had a son that she left, day after day after day, because she had to, and so she would fasten her hair in barrettes and gather her books to go teach other people's children.

My mother had a son, and once, when the mother had fastened her barrettes and gone to school to teach other people's children, the child, left at home alone, abandoned the silence of the empty house and walked into the darkest heart of the forest—each tree looking just like another—until he was completely lost and could not find his way home again. The child was practicing, even at this early age, to always find the safe path back. He tried every path before he discovered that there were no safe paths.

My mother had a son, and when the son grew up old enough to want to prove his independence, the son told a story about walking unsupervised into the wilderness and never finding his way out, and the mother cried and cried until there were no tears left to give the son.

My mother had a son, and the son was bookish and introverted, because there was solace within books, and he learned that a book would never leave you.

My mother had a son, and although it took years, he finally grew old enough that he didn't care when she left.

My mother had a son who learned not to show that he cared, although anyone who was watching would have seen his sad eyes from behind the blinds in the living room window as he watched the mother drive away and disappear.

My mother had a son who looked for second mothers everywhere his eyes fell, mothers who wouldn't leave him. But they always did.

My mother had a son who looked for girls with motherly habits.

My mother had a son who never learned to love women. He never trusted them, afraid that they would always leave him, like the mother, who always felt guilty but always left anyway, because by the time the truth was understood, the damage was already done.

My mother had a son who loved women too much. He became a serial monogamist, moving from one woman to another woman, always looking for something he couldn't define or explain but knowing that what he found was never it.

My mother had a son who loved women too much. He stopped believing in monogamy.

My mother had a son who didn't love women enough.

How the Son Loved

The son fell in love over and over.

The son went to the city, where the sky was held up by concrete skyscrapers, and fell in love with women who wore thigh-high leather boots. He wanted to peel the boots off the women and make love to them in uptown hotel rooms, and there were many with whom he did make love in uptown hotel rooms and also shitty efficiency apartments and sometimes in the alleys behind dance clubs where the music beat so loud that it almost blocked the smell of the garbage.

The son went to the city and fell in love with the concrete and the skyscrapers, and he forgot about places where mountains held up the sky without the need of concrete, and he never went home.

The son went into the country, where the sky was held up by mountains, and fell in love with a teacher, who fastened her hair with barrettes like his mother, and when he made love to her, he pretended the barrettes did not remind him of his mother.

The son stayed home all of his life and never fell in love at all.

The son fell in love with gears and machinery. The son fell in love with mechanics.

The son fell in love with a mechanic and spent his nights smelling skin stained with oil and grease and the hard chemical smell of soap that removed the dirt but never the evidence of its existence.

The son fell in love with a man just like his father and spent his life trying to please him but never succeeding.

The son fell in love with a teacher and a mechanic. He married one and fucked the other.

The son fell in love with the mountains and the trees, because they were more dependable than the men and women he could not fall in love with, and he built a house in the country, where he learned the calls of cattle in the darkness, such as when a mother calls her calf to suck.

The son fell in love with books and the words inside books and the characters the books were about, so much so that he never learned to fall in love with a real person who breathed independently of an author's desire, whose heart might bleed in time with his own.

The son fell in love with the whole world, and the weight of it was too much for any heart, much less one as weak and damaged and essentially human as his own.

Z. E. Ratches
The Stem

The advent of time travel was far less dramatic than all the old science fiction movies and comic books had led us to believe. Mainly because you could only go three minutes into the past and only for 33 seconds. It was a novelty. A gadget to buy to say you had it. As with most modern gadgets, Apple developed the first one. They, predictably, called it iTime. It looked like a thinner, longer iPad and cost about as much. Also predictably, Google came out with a cheaper, better version about six months later. They called it Google Time and it sent you back 33 minutes where you stayed for about three and a half minutes. A few third party developers got involved after that, their scientists and engineers tinkering until they eventually developed the current models that can take you back exactly three days from the present where you linger for 33 minutes.

Scientists seem pretty convinced this is the furthest they'll ever be able to send us. Travel into the future is still not possible and has hit a roadblock so big, no one is really working on it anymore. The limit on how far back we can travel has to do with the nature of time, the realization of which was the catalyst for the discovery of time travel. Time is a part of our physical world and not just a concept. Before, we had only really been able to measure time, but now, we are beginning to analyze and quantify it as a part of physical space. However, there is a limit. Just as mass is theorized to turn into energy at a certain speed, time becomes rigid the longer it sits. Time begins almost fluid and then hardens the longer it exists. It makes me wonder if time in the far past is brittle. Maybe it falls away. Perhaps that is the beginning or ending of a universe.

So now, a person can travel exactly three days into the past for 33 minutes. When they return, it is 33 minutes ahead of when they left, so you can't just go back to the same 33 minutes over and over again. The time is constantly hardening; the wall is constantly pushing us forward. This, of course, takes some of the fun out of time travel. No one can go back in time and kill Hitler or find out if Jesus was really a magical deity or just a nice Jewish kid with a hammer. And there are other disappointments that come with such short distances in time travel than just not being able to do all the things people theorize about while high. More personal disappointments. Time travel inspired a yearning for further time travel because now, people's secret desires were tantalizingly within reach.

Thoughts ranging from:

"I would have done high school so differently."

"I wouldn't have married my first or third husband."

"I would have majored in something besides philosophy. Shit, did he say he wanted fries with that?"

To:

"I would stop myself from getting in that car."

"I would tell her I love her one more time."

"I would have had the abortion."

Unintentionally, time travel had caused regrets to deepen and a frustration with time had developed. No one could "let come what may" anymore, although some of us never could. So really, everyone was just contracting the neurosis some of us had wrapped ourselves in way earlier than three days ago. Too far back to fix.

Traveling through time is a very confusing and disorienting experience. It's not like in the movies. You don't get into a DeLorean and travel back and have fun adventures you remember your whole life. In fact, most time travel no one remembers vividly at all. Everyone has tried the same experiment at least once:

Step 1. Your friend stands right in front of you with their device.

Step 2. They say, "Ok, don't take your eyes off me; don't even blink!"

Step 3. You say, "I won't! I won't!" and you both have this wild, exuberant look in your eyes. You're going to do it. You'll be the first to watch and actively remember time travel. You're going to experience it just like Hollywood had portrayed in the movies.

Step 4. Your friend presses the button.

The result of this experiment is always the same. There's a fuzzy shift and then your friend is there, but you don't really remember if they were gone or where they went. It's like when you're walking down a road and feeling someone behind you and eventually they catch up, and your friend is walking next to you and it isn't startling because you felt her coming, but you can't really say precisely when she arrived. And it always happens like that. No one has reported a clear, lucid, sequential experience of watching someone travel back and forth in time. When you're in the past, everything is crystal clear for the person traveling. But then, when you phase back, everything contains just a faint hint of being off-balance. Your vision is blurry and you're a little dizzy and then everything stabilizes and you don't really know where you were or what you did but the device is in your hand. After a few times you know that feeling means you were traveling. The only way I know things are clear when someone is in the past is by capturing first-hand experiences from people who have traveled. They say that to them, everything is moving like reality should. Of course, I don't know how many of them I've talked to because the memory of them fades after a few weeks.

That's how we know it works though, because there are people from the future around us all the time. One of my favorite time traveler encounters was last week, and I hope the humor pins it in my brain so it becomes a lasting memory, but I don't really know how it works. Maybe we just forget everyone if they aren't there to constantly remind us. I was in the produce section at the grocery store and this guy kept looking at me. He was flashing me the *look-how-charming-I-can-be-with-just-a-single-glance* eyes. I was debating whether I was going to give up on my pursuit of the cute stock guy for this new more receptive conquest when an exact copy of him ran in and whispered something in his ear. His eyes grew really wide. He dropped his basket in the middle of the aisle and ran out with his future self. I just chuckled and thought, *What could I have possibly done in three days, anyway?*

Another experience I had a while back that I will always remember was a fight between my mother and I (because, of course, any scientific breakthrough can be used by angsty teenagers to cause conflict). It was back in high school and I had gotten a really, really terrible hair cut. I pleaded with my mother to let me stay home from school:

"I can't go like this!" I wailed, "Everyone will make fun of me! Just let me stay home from school for the next three days and then I'll go back, tell myself not to get the hair cut, and then I'll go to school these three days. So, in reality, I will have gone during the three days off."

My mother replied, "No, you'll go to school these three days, and then if you go back and change it, you'll forget all about the teasing. Maybe the faint hint of character built in you by the adversity will linger."

"That's literally dumb," I said, which was the height of my capacity for cogent debate at the time. In the end, I went to school those three days and then, on the third day, I was busy and forgot to travel back in time. Everything worked out; I figured out a way to style it so it wasn't so heinous, I guess.

The existence of time travel also added a whole new layer to common, everyday experiences. Deja vu went from a weird feeling to a proven possibility. The disorienting effects made this even more profound. Have I done this before? Did I get hit by that truck? How did it play out? How did I handle it? Well obviously not well because I came back to change it. Do I know him from somewhere?

The concept of reality has changed for me around all of this. The best way I can visualize what is happening to time is like a tomato plant. There is a main stock and it grows these fine hairs from the bottom up. These hairs are actually roots. If the stock is cut, and a portion with these hairs is planted, it'll grow into a whole other plant. But more often than not, they just sit there and eventually wilt away and fall off. So, time has a main line running along space, but now that we've discovered time travel there are these other little stocks of realities that existed but weren't allowed to form roots. They have the same origin, but only one continues to grow while the others just stay as faint possibilities tethered to the larger stem: the present that *is*. These roots are like u-turns. They are reality but not *this* reality. They are made from this reality and would have occurred had we not turned back. Are we just the cut of a stock of the cut of a stock of the...you get the picture.

All of these faint alternate realities make me wonder what will happen as we continue to use this technology. These pasts are real and actually happened, but they are like echoes following you through life. Other people and other things would be in the same spot I am if a different root had taken hold. And as we go back more and more, the number of echoes and shadows increases and the number of physical possibilities existing in each and every space grows. How long will it be until the sheer amount of the tiny sucker roots makes them weigh more than the stem? How long until the echoes drown out the voice? How long until reality becomes a piece of paper that has been written on and erased from so many times that it becomes too thin and crumpled and all that is on it is a smudge of graphite and the chaos of impressions left by millions of pencils? How long until...

Wait, what was I saying?

Mary Skomerza

The Imminent Widow

The outline of his shadow gyrates and roils against the wall, a disturbing pantomime of respiration. His breaths, raspy and uneven, heave upwards with a rumble and deflate with a hiss. It is an oddly hypnotic symphony. I watch him with waning energy, sinking lower into my seat while my eyes flutter against the weight of my lashes. There is a smell about him that I hadn't noticed before. It thickens the air with a medicinal putrid odor. I drift into an uneasy slumber.

During interludes of stillness in my fitful rest I dream that a giant centipede climbed up into the sky and wrapped itself around the sun. It tightened its coil until the last ray of light was pinched out and we were left looking at that high-up bug, all legs upon spines. It looks like a tumor, or a desolate planet.

I slum around hospitals and pharmaceutical counters. I grip edges with hands that are slick with a sweat more viscous than liquid, a constant stickiness that oozes out of my pale nervous skin. The nurse behind the desk looks at me with a concerned, downturned brow. She's not sure why I'm still here. I look for the nervous young doctor who told us, fiddling with his prescription pad, that the best thing we could do is keep him comfortable. I had half-expected him to write us a script for throw pillows. The fluorescents wash over the waiting room with a bone-white light, cast harshly like the desert sun. Death under these lights is clean. It looks phony, like a well-rehearsed tragedy of repeated performances.

Set the scene: the imminent widow in unwashed clothes clings to a chipped white desktop. She is surrounded by hospital patrons in vinyl chairs crusted with grief. Someone waiting in the corridor lets out a scream and is hushed. The young doctor enters stage left, sighing at the sight of the ghost in the calico dress who propels herself towards him, a trail of pennies behind her falling from her deteriorating pocketbook.

"He was vomiting last night," I tell him.

He leans behind me and begins picking up the change off the tile.

"That's to be expected," he says.

He's down on one knee, palming the coins one at a time.

"He's just so tired, all the time. I need something to give him, to make him feel a little better."

He stands and shakes his head with a forced solemnity. The coins make a sound like a muffled bell ringing as the doctor deposits them into my hand.

The doctor tries not to look at the ghost who slithers anxiously inside her oversized dress as he apologizes to her. He's unnerved by the woman whose hands are so cold, like she lives in an icebox, but whose eyebrows are streaked with a glistening banner of sweat. He mumbles another apology and exits stage left. The ghost lightens a shade. She gets harder to see every passing day. The nurse calls out a name and a coughing man pulls himself slowly out of his chair. The woman who calls herself a ghost disappears off stage, walks past the audience and through the theater doors. End scene.

I've forgotten how to have conversations. I try to think of them like tennis matches. Your turn, my turn. But someone will say something to me and I will draw a blank on what to say in return. They skip my turn and say something else. What do I do then? Do I go twice? Do I respond to the first comment or the second? Are redos allowed?

So I rarely talk anymore, at least not the way I used to. Words come out haltingly, with a practiced monotony of syllables. Stones round their edges with wear. So do words.

"Fine… thank… you."

My speech is slightly slurred, spoken with a fat tongue. I am not drunk. Just weary.

Her turn: "How's Ed?"

My turn: "Bad."

Her turn: "In a lot of pain?"

Nod. Slap the tennis ball back to her. Sneaky move. No words, just a twitch of the neck.

Her turn: "I know someone. She does, um, alternative medicine. Holistic, herbal."

Shit. What now? Keep nodding.

Her: "I'll give you her information."

Nod.

Her: "You should give her a try."

Me: …

* * *

I dream that the centipede unfurls himself and begins slinking across the sky, dropping his front end down every once in a while to snatch someone with his thorny mandible. I wake up to see if Ed is still breathing. It's too dark to see him. I prod around for the ridges of his rib cage and lay my hand across his chest. There is still warmth emanating from him. It's warmth that comes with a stench; sulfuric fumes of life slowly evaporating, joining with the molecules in the air and absorbing into the things around us. I make a waving motion with my hands trying to fan the fumes back into him, persuading with the tips of my fingers the life to reabsorb into his body. It's not working. The fumes are evasive.

The morning is spitefully bright. The city bus lurches forward and with seemingly great effort rumbles down the street. It moves with a feebleness that strikes me as overly dramatic. A young mother sitting across from me attempts half-heartedly to calm her writhing baby. She leans back with a defeated arrangement of features and closes her eyes. The baby sounds off like a foghorn. I count the blocks but lose tally when the bus driver begins shouting things over the intercom.

Her house constitutes a high slab of masonry; white, unfriendly, industry stucco. There are bars on the windows. It is a row house, pressed intimately against the shoulders of flanking neighbors. I rap hollowly against the door. My knock rings vacantly and I worry it's not audible from inside. Worries abate when the door swings open, emitting a metal whine of rusted hinges.

There is a savageness about her. Not in her features though, which curve fluidly and are accented by arabesque-like deeply folded lines. Her wrinkles look purposefully carved. The only disarray about her is her hair, grown long, matted and wiry. She looks spectral.

We two ghosts take a moment to look at each other. I mention the friend I have, who is strange and dismissive of convention but reliable, and perceive a flicker of recognition in the woman's eyes. I try to let her know, in every which way but the most direct, how desperate I am. I ring my hands like a worried mother, mostly absentmindedly. She reaches out and wraps her fingers around my squirming tic, holding me still. I feel suddenly fragile and embarrassed. I want to cry but feel like I don't know how.

I envision her as my mother as she pulls me inside. We are younger and I am whimpering. She chides me for playing where I shouldn't have. She tells me she's going to slap the insides of my arms with a wooden spoon for not listening to her. I know she won't. Mother was a half-assed disciplinarian.

The old woman looks at me with dilated, owl-like eyes. I wonder fleetingly if she's on hallucinogens. She gives me a predatory look and drags me into the kitchen. Her house is tidy, oddly normal. Where are the curare darts? I wonder.

"I came here in secret," I tell her.

She guides me into a chair. It has a concave wicker bottom. It squeaks.

"People'd think I was crazy to visit you. A *shaman*?"

She puts a kettle on the stove. Copper on electric. There's a bowl of dried rosemary and sage on the counter. A cat sleeps in the corner.

"Maybe I'm crazy, but not for that reason."

I notice an ectoplasm glaze to her eyes. She's too calm for this situation.

"No, not crazy. Just sleep deprived."

Jesus, say *something*, I want to tell her. You're making me sound batty. Bubble, bubble, toil and trouble. Take me to your tent. We can chew on some chicory root.

The kettle whistles, loud as a singing machine gun and startles me. I sit, shell-shocked, for a minute. She brews me some tea. She's awfully lithe for her age. Narrow fingers dip herb-swollen cheesecloth into hot water.

Calms the nerves.

I can barely hear her when she talks. For a moment I think that disembodied whisper is my own. Her voice is soft. It ripples the air politely, insignificantly. I watch for the movement of her lips so I will know when she is talking and when it's just the murmuring air.

She pivots towards the counter and clears her throat. From behind a curtain of knotted hair she rattles off the names of several herbs she grows in the lot behind her house. Good for fever, good for indigestion. The cat rubs against my leg and I nearly leap out of my chair. She turns and looks at me squarely, following the shift of my cagey gaze.

I can sense something about her. She's got healing vibes, more than that jumpy doctor. He had displaced intentions, not enough experience. I clap my hands together. Tea dribbles over the side of a mug.

"Okay, witch. Who must we curse?"

It must take a dark magic to catch someone fallen from the brink, I presume. Give me the mythical squirming worm who slurps tumors with a fleshy proboscis. The cells have staged a coup. Discipline them. Fix him.

I can't.

Was it the breeze that spoke?

"Nonsense. Give me the potion. I will administer it myself."

I can't help him.

Well then what the hell good are you? If all you have is your kettle! Leaves and water… Goes down easy but stings in the gut. You poisonous charlatan. All you can offer is relief; well you and death are selling the same substance.

The imminent widow slumps in her chair. Her skin is blanched. Cellophane thin and crinkled the same way. She can't tell what she's said and what she's thought. *I can't help you.* No hope. She murmurs back. The old woman drapes her old arms across the shoulders of the weary ghost. The tea smells like lavender. She notices the house smells like lavender too.

The old woman sees me out, two light fingers on my elbow. My eyes feel raw in the sunlight. It hasn't rained in a month.

Ed wonders where I've been. I tell him I went to the pharmacy, brandishing an unopened aspirin bottle as proof. I lay my hand across his forehead. A spray of his baby fine hair tickles me as I lift my palm. He asks me to take care of myself. I pretend to not know what he means.

I dream that the centipede has taken up residence in the old woman's house. Her row house is now a façade, a ceramic curtain that lifts up to reveal a covert lair littered with syringes, buckets overflowing with creamed tumor, dried lizards pinned to the wall. The woman is nowhere to be found. I wake up. Ed, as I knew him, is gone.

I observe him. From my chair I long for him. He has a look, thin and childlike, that rakes at my heart as we sit side by side and I think of the proverbial "we" that has just dissolved and will dissolve once again when we can no longer sit side by side. I hate myself for having thought we might outlive our fondness for one another.

I hate to be alone.

I hate grief.

I hate time. But time proved to be somewhat of an illusion. A spiraling maelstrom of crying jags and dreamless sleep that continued for an unmeasured amount of time. Now is later, and I find myself at the woman's door. Tip my head up, beg for rain. Knock lightly. Even from out here, I can smell her lavender.

William Falo
Street Girl

Anton watched the people leave the gothic-style church after a rare winter wedding and felt the dull ache in his stomach spread to his heart. He blinked away the tears before they could fall.

The bookstore was emptier then usual and the loneliness became too much to bear, so he put up the closed sign. A door slammed and footsteps pounded on the sidewalk.

"Stop you pest!" someone shouted. He turned to see Radu grab a street boy, throw him to the ground, and then straddle him, lifting a clenched fist. The boy had on a blue hat that became pulled down over his ears as he squirmed to get free, but Radu had a strong grip from years of working in the market.

The punch connected with a sickening thud, and the boy let out a high-pitched wail. Anton With his arm hanging midair, ready to strike like a hammer, Radu scanned the street and locked eyes with Anton.

"Anton, come and help me. This boy robbed me again."

Anton approached the scene with hesitation. Radu swung again, his punch glancing off the boy's cheek.

"Help me," Radu said again as the boy twisted on the ground. Anton was always worried about being robbed by the street children, but they usually stayed out of his bookstore. Still, he was afraid of them.

Radu pulled his leg back and landed a kick along the helpless child's side. The boy winced, but Anton kicked him again and again until the boy released a wailing cry, tears running down his cheeks. Radu lifted his arm to strike him once more and said, "You'll never rob me again."

Anton recognized the defeat in the boy's tear-soaked face and grabbed the shop owner's fist. "No more," he said. "Let him go."

"That's fine for you to say. They constantly steal food from me." Radu straightened and released the boy, turning his attention to Anton. "They don't want your books and you have no money."

The boy dragged his broken body away with blood trickling out of his nose. His left eye was swollen and red. A long strand of black hair fell out from under the boy's hat and dangled behind him as he hobbled away and disappeared down the empty street.

Radu wiped his bloody hand on his stained shirt. "You shouldn't have stopped me."

"He was just a street kid."

"Fine for you to say. They don't steal books, but I saw you kick him."

Anton walked into the bookstore. He locked the door and went out the back entrance not wanting to see the place where he kicked the boy so many times.

A pack of stray dogs gathered outside his house in Grazoveste. The dogs were even more numerous then the street children in Romania. He would usually chase them away with curses and handfuls of rocks, but this time he just walked around them.

The dinner he made remained untouched, and he threw it outside to the dogs resulting in a noisy feeding frenzy. The TV and radio couldn't drown out the bedraggled boy's cries that ricocheted in his mind.

The store remained closed the next day while Anton lay in his bed until noon. He glanced at the picture of his wife on the end table. He stared at her pale blue eyes, made even softer by the coating of dust that had accumulated over the years.

"Why did you have to die?"

With no answers he placed the picture back. A tear fell onto her cheek. The house was filled with sorrow and he walked out toward the street.

The dogs were gone, but he knew they would return everyday for food. Gray clouds drifted across the sky threatening to bring snow. A boy walked in front of him. His clothes dragged on the ground and a nauseous glue smell came from him.

Anton followed the boy to an overgrown vacant lot. The boy carried a brown bag; Anton knew it contained the glue that the street children inhaled. He saw another boy and girl come out from behind an old shed. The taller boy reached out for the bag when the boy reached him. "Oh my God," he said. He recognized the boy as the one he had kicked. The boy inhaled deeply from the bag then stumbled backwards, his hat tumbling off his head. Long strands of the same inky hair fell across his face and shoulders and his shirt pulled tight around him.

"He's a girl," Anton said aloud.

A girl. He kicked a girl with all his might.

His mind fluttering, Anton returned to the store and stared out the front window. He saw the girl walk by towards the market across the street, and saw Radu watching from the window of the market. He dashed out the door and grabbed her arm. She reeled back and pulled a knife out.

"I just wanted to keep you away from the market. That man will kill you."

She looked back and saw Radu looking at her. "I wasn't going in there but—"

"Come in here," he pointed toward the bookstore.

"Books. No thanks. I can't eat books."

"You can have my lunch."

"How do I know you won't try anything?"

"You have a knife."

She pointed toward him. "Did you help that man beat me?"

He stood still, unable to look in her eyes. She started to cough so harshly that she doubled over. He winced when he thought of how hard he had kicked her. When she stopped coughing he gave her his lunch and a hot cup of coffee. The smell of glue from her tattered clothes filled the store. A lady opened the door, saw the girl, and then turned and left.

"I know you're a girl. What's your name?"

"Anca," she said.

She looked at the books on the shelf.

"Why did you dress as a boy?"

"So perverts stop trying to buy me or rape me. It's already happened to me enough."

He fell silent and after a moment asked, "Do you read?"

"Of course. I went to school until my mother let an alcoholic boyfriend move in. He abused me and when I complained to her she told me that I was lying. I can never go back."

She coughed again. "Are you sick?"

"I may have leukemia."

"Seriously?"

"I wouldn't joke about that. A doctor told me once in a clinic."

"Let me take you to a doctor."

"No, never. They will take me back. I was just kidding anyway."

She took a book from a shelf about a magical kingdom. She leafed through it. "You know what I like about books?"

"What's that?"

"You never know what you will find when you turn the page."

Two small street children tapped on the window and she started to leave then stopped to give the book back.

"No, keep it," he said.

Anca joined the children outside. They shuffled down the snow-covered street while he closed the store and went home. The dogs waited, and he picked up some rocks to throw at them but decided against it. The snow fell in dreamy swirls while he walked to the overgrown lot.

Two footprints led away from the place where Anca lived. They belonged to the smaller children. Why didn't she go with them? He looked inside the shed and saw her breathing erratically while her eyes stared straight ahead. The book was open on her lap. Her face shimmered from the poisonous paint they sometimes inhaled instead of glue. He felt her forehead and gasped when he realized she was burning with a fever. Her eyes rolled back and left empty white sockets.

"No," he yelled and picked her up. She flopped in his arms as he carried her through the snow for ten blocks until he reached the hospital. The nurse saw him and refused to let her in.

"She smells of glue or paint. I know she's a street kid. We don't take them here. If we take one then they all will come."

"My God. I will pay for her."

"Fine," she said, a suspicious glint in her eye. They placed her on a gurney and rolled her into the back. He held her cold hand. They gave him many forms to fill and asked questions he didn't know the answers to. Then an alarm rang. The shrill sound brought people running and they surrounded her after pushing him out of the way.

He watched in shock and prayed for help. Suddenly, it became too quiet and the doctor approached him with a gave expression, and when he shook his head, Anton collapsed to his knees and wept. They had to escort him out of the hospital after a few hours. Nothing seemed the same. His heart was broken. The sound of the kicks to a dying girl's side echoed through his mind.

The lot was covered with snow and he approached the shed slowly. The boy and girl stood inside beside a small fire they started in a can. The pages of the book burned in the flames sending smoke up toward heaven.

"Hello," he said. They both turned and tensed.

"Anca is dead."

"No," they both yelled. "She went home. She'll be back later."

He shook his head and sobbed. "Get out," the boy punched him in the stomach. Grunting from the force of the small boy's attack, Anton turned and left the children in a requiem of silence.

He went to the store and began clearing out his belongings. A "For Sale" sign was hung in the window. He could never open it again after the girl died and what he had done to her right in front of it. He stared outside and saw the two little children walking down the street. They went into the market and then ran out with a pack of cookies. Radu ran after them and grabbed the boy. Anton moved with lightning speed and grabbed Radu's arm forcing him to release the boy. Then he pushed him back against the wall. "Don't touch them."

"Are you crazy?"

"Just leave them alone. Here take this." He shoved money at Radu then pushed him away. The children watched, and backed away in fear.

"Wait, come in here. You can have my lunch."

They followed him in. "Books," they both said.

"They can be more interesting if you read them instead of burning them. Anytime you want one you can come here even if you do just burn them."

He walked through the cemetery with a bunch of flowers. The snow crunched under his feet and he knelt before her grave. He placed the flowers on it.

"Don't worry. I promise I'll look after your friends. They'll never be alone and you won't either. I will come every day. I'm so sorry that I hurt you." He collapsed on the blanket of snow, and cried.

His tears fell onto the flowers where they froze and shimmered in the light. He felt a gentle touch on his shoulder and it comforted him. When he turned he saw a page of a book on his arm.

His hand shook when he saw that it came from the same book that he had given Anca and then he pressed it to his heart.

Back at the bookstore he saw a street child walk by with black hair dangling from underneath a hat. He ran outside but knew it couldn't be her and slumped against the wall.

Radu swept the sidewalk, a menacing look carved on his face. He pointed at two street children walking toward the store. "Look what you started."

Anton turned and smiled when he saw the boy and girl walk into the bookstore. He removed the "For Sale" sign and, tucking it under his arm, followed them inside.

Mort Castle

Altenmoor, Where the Dogs Dance

One day in spring, when the boy came home from school, he did not find Rusty in the backyard, on the screened-in porch, or anywhere downstairs in the house. He knew Rusty could not be up with Grandpa. Last winter, when the weather had gone so cold, Rusty's back legs had gone cold, too, so cold he could no longer climb the stairs.

The boy's mother took him into the kitchen and tried to explain, though he hadn't asked her. "Rusty's gone, Marky."

He hated being called "Marky," but she was his mom, so what could he do? Dad called him "Mark," and sometimes "Son," and that was better but it still wasn't right.

Grandpa knew and always called him "Boy." He felt like a "boy," not "Mark," or "Son," or (phoo!) "Marky!" Once in a while he wondered if that would change when he got older.

Mom said Rusty was very old. In a dog way, Rusty was more than a hundred. She said Rusty had had a very good life because everyone loved him a lot, and now Rusty's life was over.

The way Mom talked made the boy think she was trying not to frighten him. Then she hugged him so hard all his air rushed out and he thought Mom was trying not to be frightened, too.

But the boy didn't understand, so he said, "I'll go see Grandpa." Grandpa knew how to talk about things so the boy understood because Grandpa was very smart. He was so smart that long ago, when he could still see, Grandpa even used to write books.

"He'll like that," Mom said. "Go see him."

Upstairs at the end of the hall, across from his own room, the boy knocked on Grandpa's door. He waited one-two-three, then heard Grandpa say, "Enter." Grandpa always made him wait one-two-three, never one, or one-two, or one-two-three-four.

Grandpa sat in a straight-backed chair by the window. Grandpa didn't have a rocking chair and the boy knew why because once Grandpa had told him. "Old people are supposed to sit in rockers. Seldom in life have I done the 'supposed to's.'"

Through the window, the sun shone a square of light at Grandpa's feet. The boy stood with his sneakers at the edge of the square. If he stepped inside, it might break, the yellow ozzing out like the yolk of a poached egg.

The boy said, "Grandpa, Mom says Rusty is gone."

"Your mother is truthful enough," Grandpa said, "though so sadly lacking in imagination it's often difficult for me to acknowledge her as my daughter."

"Oh," the boy said. Sometimes Grandpa talked funny, except he never did when he was talking about important things—like Altenmoor.

"Mom says Rusty was very old," the boy said.

"Indeed," Grandpa said.

"You're very old."

"Once more, indeed."

The boy remembered when Grandpa had been old, but not very old. Grandpa got very old when the cloudy-looking white film covered his eyes. After that, Grandpa couldn't read anymore, not even the Altenmoor books Grandpa had written himself.

"I'll miss that too, Boy," Grandpa said. "The picture of Rusty asleep and the sound of his adenoidal snore are preserved and treasured in my memory."

Grandpa tipped his head. For a second the boy thought Grandpa wasn't blind at all because the boy could almost feel himself being seen. "Do say on, Boy," Grandpa said.

"Is Rusty dead?" the boy said.

Grandpa said, "There are some who would say and some who would believe it as well. And you? What do you say? What do you believe?"

The boy thought. Then he said, "No."

"No?"

"Rusty went to Altenmoor," the boy said and he hoped he believed what he was saying. "He went once through the Rubber Tree Woods and he jig-jogged left past the Marmalade Mound. Then he followed the winding Happy-To-You River to Altenmoor."

"Continue, Boy." Grandpa leaned forward, elbows on his knees, hands folded under his chin. "Speak to me of Altenmoor. So long since I've written of the noble realm and longer still since I've gone a-journeying there."

"In Altenmoor, every morning is a Sunrise Surprise and the buttercups thunder like twelve tubas."

"Only louder," Grandpa said.

"Much louder! And the winds are all hot winds and happy winds and wild winds!"

"And the animals?"

"Oh," the boy said, remembering the animals. "The pigs whistle 'Dixie' in four-part harmony and the cats play silver cymbals in three-quarter time."

"And the dogs?"

"The dogs dance!" the boy said. "The dogs do dance all the day!"

"You see," Grandpa said, "it was time for Rusty to be where the dogs dance. Yes. Rusty has gone to Altenmoor."

The boy smiled but the smile didn't feel all the way right because it pinched at the corners of his mouth, and so he had to ask. "Really?"

"'Really?' The modern rephrasing of the ageless 'What is Truth?' The metaphysicians ponder as they will, all we truly know, we know only here." Grandpa patted himself on the chest.

The boy said, "There is a real Altenmoor?"

"Were there not, could I have written the seventeen books that comprise the complete Altenmoor chronicles? If there were no Oz, could Mr. L. Frank Baum have related the adventures of Dorothy and Tin Woodsman and Scarecrow? What of Treasure Island and Never-Neverland, or savage Pellucidar and Wonderland? If they did not exist, how could people tell of them?"

Again Grandpa patted himself on the chest. "Books, boy, are from the heart and of teh heart. That makes them not merely true, but truer than true. Do you understand?"

"Some," the boy said. "Not everything."

"Some is more than most people," Grandpa said. "It will suffice."

The boy had something else to ask. "But how could Rusty get to Altenmoor, Grandpa? It's a long, long way and his legs were no good."

Grandpa stretched out his arm and spread his fingers. In the sunlight the veins of his hand were ripply blue and strong. "I touched Rusty's head, you see. I patted that bony knob at the back of his skull and tickled between his ears. I touched him, and all the strength I could give, I gave to Rusty so he could make the trek to Altenmoor."

"And then he went?"

"He did," Grandpa said. "He went once through the Rubber Tree Woods and he jig-jogged left past the Marmalade Mound."

"Then he followed the winding Happy-To-You River to Altenmoor!" the boy and grandpa said together.

"Yes," Grandpa nodded, "and now Rusty is dancing, he is dancing where the dogs dance. I believe that."

"I do too," the boy said.

On a winter night so cold that the house could not keep out all the winter chill, the boy awoke. He thought at first that a dream had frightened him awake, but he realized he was not frightened.

Then he knew it was a thought that had pulled him from his sleep.

He got out of bed. Even through the carpet the floor was shivery, so he slid his feet along istead of lifting them. He did not need a light. He stepped across the hall and quietly knocked on the door. It would have been wrong to wake Mom and Dad. They did not mind getting up if he had a stomachache or a bad dream, but his stomach felt fine and he was not dreaming.

The boy waited one-two-three.

Then he waited four and five and six and seven before he gently turned the knob and went in.

"Grandpa?" The boy stood beside the bed, thinking one-two-three-four-five-six.

Then the boy thought about what he would miss about Grandpa, things he wanted to keep in his memory. There were a lot of things, and once he was sure he had them all, the boy touched the back of Grandpa's hand, then took hold of three of Grandpa's fingers and squeezed.

Grandpas' eyes opened. Beneath the milky glaze his eyes looked right at the boy, and this time the boy was almost certain Grandpa could see him.

"Yes? What is it, Boy?"

"Are you going to Altenmoor now?" the boy said. Slowly Grandpa sat up. "Yes, I believe I am."

"Then I have to help you."

"Yes." Grandpa nodded. "Keep hold of my hand, Boy."

The boy did. It took a long time, but he could feel himself giving all the strength he could give to Grandpa. He knew it was happening because he started to feel as though he were going to sleep, the way he did in the back of the car after a long day at the beach.

Then Grandpa said, "Thank you," and took away his hand.

"Grandpa, will you go now?"

"Shortly." Grandpa said. "No longer than it takes a pig to whistle 'Dixie.' Now you must return to bed. There is still much of a winter's night to sleep away."

"Okay," the boy said. He went to the door, then stopped and looked back. "Grandpa, you know. The Rubber Tree Woods and the Marmalade Mound and the winding Happy-To-You River."

"Of course, Boy," Grandpa said. "Where else?"

The boy said, "Goodbye, Grandpa."

The next morning the boy was up early because his mother and father came to his room and woke him and told him he wouldn't be going to school. Dad stood by the door. He had the same look on his face he'd had when someone stole the car last year.

Mom held the boy close to her. She was crying.

She said, "Grandpa is gone, Marky."

"Yes," the boy said. He wished he could explain but he knew she would never understand.

Mike McCorkle

The Sound

"Who's there?" the old man yelled from his kayak. An oppressive silence overcame him like a wave. He was not a man to hear voices in the night nor go to church on Sunday, but how can he deny the haunting, audible intonation?

Beware.

The sinister voice warned him as the boat crested over the first waves he met on the two nautical-mile, open-water crossing. He wondered for a moment if his mind was truly escaping him. Madness, however subjective, he rarely deferred to. In solitude noises can be explained away as the consequences of isolation. Despite his predilection to heed the plea of this sound, the old man continued, dismissing the warning as an encroachment of his imagination.

The glass surface broke open, spilling its perfectly symmetric ripples across the seawater. Rhythmically, the bow of the kayak cut through the long strands of kelp reaching for the surface like drowned men stretching for salvation. The old man drove his hand-carved Inuit paddle deep into the frigid waters of the Puget Sound, each stroke carrying him farther from a world he no longer belonged. In the Sound he found solace in the perfect equilibrium of nature. Only the soft acoustic song of the water rolling along his *baidarka*[1] could be heard. The wind wisped across his menacing white beard as he led himself along the tidal currents that flowed out to the distant Pacific. Leaving the bay, the harbor seals barked their solemn goodbyes.

Referring to the nautical map kept rubber-banded to the deck of his vessel, he plotted a course straight one nautical mile to shore at the next island for a respite. While scratching the last red wax pencil marks across the laminate surface of the map, the light from the sun was swallowed behind him. The old sailors chapped mouth fell wide as his pale blue eyes surmised the enormous wall of fog that was rolling towards him at 15 knots. Fog is perhaps the most dangerous hazard a small sea kayak could encounter on the Sound; with the shipping lanes that bear massive cargo-freighters to and from Seattle, it steals any visibility for avoiding catastrophe. In a panic, the old man drove on with a determined ferocity in each stroke, fighting to reach the shore before the fog engulfed him. He could not escape his fate.

The fog swallowed him in its gray, endless abyss. Decidedly, he kept on as straight as possible, stretching for shore in hopes of waiting out the sea's blinding mist. The old man paddled and paddled for what seemed like hours with no indication he was nearing his destination. And as he hopelessly struggled against the emptiness of the fog, the sun extinguished itself, ushering in complete darkness.

---

1   A *baidarka* is a traditional Inuit kayak made of skin or canvas tightly wrapped around a cedar frame.

In the emptiness of night, the water stilled to a calm with no measurable sense of current. The old man's kayak floated in the wastelands as he listened in agony to the silence. He could hear the beating of his heart in the vacuity of all sound and matter. Bum-bum bum-bum bum-bum, his heart resounded. It was so clear, and audible; its pulses vibrated across his aged and weathered skin. From his dazed exhaustion, the old man startled alert at the realization that it was not the sound of his heart beating. It was the sound of drums.

In the distance he could hear a steady tribal chorus pounding away a rhythmic beat. It was constant and ominous, spilling its shadowy tendrils of sound into the darkness. He knew that it was his only viable choice. The temperature plummeted, and in the fog, he was truly lost. He drew his paddle deep and turned to face the drums. As he stroked towards the unknown, the drum's vibrations kissed his wind-chilled cheeks.

Nearer to the sound of beating drums, a large silhouette became visible in the foggy horizon. At first glance, all he could make out was an enormous black shape towering in the distance. But as the kayak coursed forward, he realized he was staring at an island. It was unfamiliar to him immediately. Coming into view were large jagged rocks, stabbing out of the sea and shore like massive splintered horns. To the east, under the moonlight he could see a large cliff face that appeared to wrap its way around the edge of the island. To the west, there was a rocky beach shadowed by a wood of straggly evergreens. While the old man slowly navigated into the shallower waters of the tidal zone, the drums began to echo louder and faster. Scanning the shore for a place to pull in, he noticed a large 40-foot pole midway along the beach. The water seemed clear near the pole, so he decided to pull in at the landmark. When he placed his left foot on the sandy shore to exit his craft, the drums stopped.

On the beach, the old sailor dragged his craft away from the tide lines in the sand and nearer to the shadowed monument that drew him there. From his boat he walked to take a closer inspection of the pole. He found that it was pitch black, as if burnt or painted in ash. From the base to the top, intricate carvings hidden by shadow covered its entire length. It was obviously a totem pole of some type. The fog parted its curtain to reveal the pale-white glow of the moon, and under its light he could make out the design. Twisted, disfigured crows stacked one upon another had been carved into the giant log. All of them had empty eye sockets, and they were pecking and tearing at one another's flesh and feathers. At the top of the pole was a carving of a man, writhing in pain, engulfed by the flock.

This was not the work of the Salish tribes that once called the waters of the Puget Sound their sanctuary. It was evil in nature and spoke fear to the heart of the old man. The object itself was so wicked in design that its pretense preceded any need for understanding. The air became cold and the night fell silent. This time it was not drums, but his heartbeat throbbing out of his chest, sending blood in painful volumes to his extremities. Only one thought played over and over in his mind. He needed to leave. The fog was safer than whatever evil baited him here.

Turning on his heels, the old man made for his boat. But before he could take comfort in escaping this nightmarish beach, an awful realization slammed his senses: his kayak was gone. Tears welled in his eyes and cascaded down his cheeks until they became snared in his beard. His craft had vanished without a trace into the night to unknown forces. Emotions surged inside of him, fueling his sense of imminent danger.

Whether it was the fear of the crows on the totem pole or

whatever had stolen his kayak from the shore, the old man decided to work his way inland in an effort to distance himself from the terrors that lurked on the island's periphery Each step across the dry, pine needle-laden forest floor sent out an echo into the darkness. He could not see farther then his own hands in front of him. Moonlit branches of wax-tipped evergreens signaled a lonely greeting in the night as he passed below. The old man was certain now that for the last twenty minutes or so, something had been following him delicately.

Every ten paces, he would pause slightly mid-step to hear a gentle footfall against the fir needles and pine branches before he placed down his own boot. It was the familiar game of the predator stalking its prey, decisively waiting to make its next move. This thing, whatever it was, followed him endlessly into the night as if he was a bleeding doe.

In a moment of blind panic, the old man bolted through the trees. With the effort of a man half his age, he pushed off into a sprint. Branches slapped against his face and cut at his skin as he passed through without concern for anything but his pursuer. He could hear it crashing behind him, crushing branches and tearing up earth in chase. His adrenaline was now fully administered and the movement below his torso became surreal as he blundered forward through the trees. Warm blood trickled across his cheek streaming from a wound on his brow. A branch had torn across his fragile skin leaving a moderate gash. The metallic taste touched his lips, but adrenaline blocked his concern.

It's gaining on me. The sounds of its steps reared closer, like feathers flapping against another paired with the crushing vibrations of large feet slamming the earth in chase. Nearer to him now, a snarling and raspy intake of air could be heard. But he could smell salt in the air and taste it on his breath. He knew he was drawing towards the shore. The horizon of dark shadowed trees seemed to thin into a staggered collection of evergreens. He could feel his legs begin to shake and weaken, but the hope of escaping this horrific thing drove him onward. The small native *salal*[2] plants brushed his legs as he ran from the last mangled branches of the wood onto the rocky open beach.

The old man quickly looked around him to evaluate where he was on the shoreline. Incredibly, his beloved kayak sat dragged up from the water a hundred yards from his location. He ran to it in a fury, slipping across the rocks as he made his way back to escape. He realized he couldn't hear the loud clambering and wheezing sounds from his pursuer anymore. He turned to look behind him for some sign of it, but saw only the dark of the forest. When his steps carried him the last few feet to his craft he realized that this, in fact, was the same shore he landed on hours before.

He glanced in every direction, searching for the totem pole, but the monument of terror was gone. It had vanished without a trace. He couldn't find any evidence proving that it had existed at all. The soil where he remembered it standing appeared unchanged. And what was even more unsettling was that he could make out his old footprints in the sand leading up to where it had stood. He traced the indents his feet had left behind, pockmarks upon the sand, until they disappeared into the forest. He looked out towards the expanse of cold salt water. The fog was gone.

The old man's mind was a turbulent sea of troubles and confusion. Exhaling a sigh of relief, he resolved to defer this encounter to madness. All that mattered to him now was he was safe and that he was leaving this damned island. He slipped his hips into the cockpit, and using his knuckles, he pushed the kayak

---

2   A native species of shrub that grows naturally in the Pacific North West.

into the icy Puget Sound. The cold water ebbing against his hands startled him. He could feel the sting of salt water as it splashed his cuts and scrapes. And as his long boat fully entered the water, he felt it begin again. Against his skin, the vibrations of a resounding chorus.

The sound of drums.

Star Spider

How Can We Ever Be Better?

He blew into town on the breeze, light as a feather, his dangling limbs thin as twigs. We watched as he passed through the streets of our town in the thick golden twilight, face obscured in the shadow of a black-rimmed hat. We whispered behind our hands, eyes narrow with a cold curiosity, sheltered as we were. He took up residence in that husk of an abandoned cottage, the one by the old cannery. Its thatching was spotty as a bald man, walls black as sin, windows slowly closing eyes. He went on in and vanished like a magic trick as the sun extinguished itself in a stuttering haze over the softly sloping hills beyond. We talked that night till the stars blazed bright and then dark again. Our words weren't wise but worried, our hands knitting our scarves and sweaters into tighter and tighter knots until they wouldn't come undone no matter how hard we pulled. Our rocking chairs made fissures into the floor, deep abyssal chasms, and our words slapped the windows like rain, so hard our children hid under their blankets for fear of lightning. Visiting strangers was unheard of in our town. It wasn't heard of and it wasn't wanted, no.

Come morning, the cottage was gleaming as though it had always stood so proud, as though its roof had never sagged or its walls had never met a lick of flame. We crowded and gawked, the butter un-churned, eggs un-gathered, harvest un-reaped or sowed. Our children faltered on the dirt road to school, bare feet anchored to the ground, lively limbs still as sleep. That breeze still blew, the one that brought the man to town, that traitorous wind now pushing a small wooden sign to and fro over the doorway of that obscenely proud cottage:

Word Lessons - Free

We hummed and hawed, how dare that man! We knew our words as well as anyone from any town from here to Timbuktu. Our children were clever, we were well spoken, we knew what we liked, and we knew what we wanted. We sputtered and sighed and turned our backs on that cottage and that man and the breeze that had brought him along. It was easy at first because he didn't make a move, didn't leave or shop or stroll. But then one morning, as we went about our business, we spotted a sign in his window:

Obsequious

We didn't understand! Our hands were covered in soil and dust and we felt disparaged. We felt small, small as the world is large because there in that window, simple as sunset, was a word we had never seen. We quieted down after that, our usually flowing waterfalls of words halting and stalling in our mouths. Then the next morning it was another word:

Unctuous

We were too proud to consult the dictionary and too angry with ourselves to make a ruckus. We had been made into fools, undone by letters, unraveled by our own ignorance.

No one was first per se, it happened all at once, like a flood where the first drop of water is never to blame. But we went, how we went, in lines like armies marching across the hills and into battle. We filled that tiny conceited cottage, paying homage to that man, bowing to him as though he were a god of letters, a king of words. He greeted us with open eyes, thin arms flung wide as though to embrace our stupidity, to transmute our common tongues into whips with which we could lash out.

We began spouting dulcet sonnets in the town square, lighting the night with our cabalistic understanding of wordplay, pontificating profusely in our bedrooms as we ravaged each other with lusty synonyms. We espoused new ideas just because we could arrange them on our lips and we felt feelings that we never knew we had because there had been no word for them before. We were liberated by our learning and we venerated the man from the cottage who smiled at us with teeth as white as precious pieces of paper.

We were ecstatic at first, of course, but then we started to slip. The small things went first, so small they weren't missed from our overflowing sentences, so small our meaning remained intact with nothing but tiny fractures in the core of the structure.

It, and, but. Our words started to run together like ink on paper not yet dry. We didn't pause, not then, not then.

I, me, we. We didn't—couldn't—stop our frenzied rapture of delirious exposition because we were too intoxicated by its delivery, drunk on the syllables that rolled off our tongues. *That, this, some, not* went next and still we didn't pause to take a breath. The tiny fractures were opening into gaping wounds, but we still couldn't see. The man, our word god, still guided us, beckoned us into his holy cottage with fingers that grew fatter and fatter by the day. His limbs and cheeks and nose were thickening like rich fudge and we were happy to see it because he had given us so much, and one who gave so much of himself deserved everything in return.

The longer words went next: *Insinuation, maledicent, ventripotent.* Like a virus spreading, our loss was a pox. For each missing noun we flushed with fever, for each missing verb we were overcome with nausea. We could not live without our words!

So violently we clawed at our throats, hoping to bring our words forth, vomit them out, spew them up from the depths of us. How callously we rutted like animals in our beds and barns, hoping to birth the words like fresh babies out into the world. But it wasn't that, it had never been that, for our fate was not in our hands. It was, of course, in the plump, fat fingers of that man-god, our teacher, our savior, well and whole in his deceitful cottage by the cannery.

When we turned on him, we had no words left, only simian grunts and howls. We were rabid creatures of flesh and rock, our children vicious as vipers in the grass. We were hunched and flawed, our knuckles dragging in the dirt, and furious, so furious, because we could still taste the perfect words on the tips of our tongues, still remember hints of the feelings, the ideas we had lost.

We approached his cottage at twilight, drawn to the scent of paper and ink as animals drawn to a fresh kill. He didn't open the door, oh no, he didn't open the door, but we bashed it down with fist and foot and rushed into that perfect place. We upended tables and paper fluttered and flew as we grabbed at it, tore into it, starving, ravenous. We ingested the words and they slid down our throats and filled our angry stomachs with consonants and vowels. The man watched from the corner, well-fed, well-spoken, a man amongst animals, a god amongst men. He tried to reason, fleshy hands raised like pale flags of surrender, words issuing like water from a broken spout. But it wasn't enough for us. We were neither man nor beast, caught in between with letters floating in our minds like ghosts haunting, haunting, but nothing more. We advanced as one large and wild creature, adults and children, one step, one mouth, one intent. He has pilfered our words, kept them for his own gluttonous pleasure, we thought. His words were useless against the seething mass of us and our hungry undulations engulfed him as he screamed and screamed those empty words into our empty ears.

We tore his flesh off first and beneath, buried in the muscle and tendon, we found our words. He had gorged on them and they had filled him, every inch of him, packed tight in thick inky clusters. We ripped them from his bones in blubbery, meaty slices. We ate and ate and our mouths were red and our fingers were red and our cheeks were flushed with rage and hunger.

Esurient, voracious, insatiable. We were endless in our obliteration, and as we ate, we returned to ourselves, our ideas, our feelings, our thoughts. We paused for breath, for words, for concern. We saw our red fingers and our children's red lips and our hair, red, and our arms, red, and everything red and inky black and we cried out. No! He stole our words, but we stole his life, how are we better? How can we ever be better? We sank into the slick stench of that damned cottage and wept red tears as the sun extinguished itself in a stuttering haze over the softly sloping hills beyond.

Frank Scozzari

Ghosts of the Villa Borghese

They stood on the Pincio Terrace, that place above the Piazza del Popolo with the commanding view of Rome. Beneath them, a thousand red-tiled rooftops stretched out across the ancient city, from the distant columns of the Coliseum to the glistening dome of St. Peters' Basilica. To the west was the long, winding curve of the Tiber River where it came around past the Castel Sant'Angelo.

"It's like we're back on the Terrace of Infinity," the young woman said.

"Yeah, but that was a little higher," Garrett replied.

"Do you think Audrey Hepburn and Gregory Peck stood here?" she asked.

"Probably."

"And Sophia Loren."

"Most likely."

"And Marcello Mastroianni and Roberto Rossellini?"

"Them too."

"Such a romantic place!"

"It is."

A warm breeze swept up from the city below and blew against their faces. In the distance they could see tiny black dots walking across plazas and sunlight flashing off the windshields of moving vehicles.

"Just think of how long this city has been here," the woman said, "...of all the many people who have come and passed."

"Probably thousands, hundreds of thousands, standing here like we are now, enjoying the same view and feeling the same warm sun."

The woman gazed thoughtfully at the horizon. "The Bernini was like a ghost, I mean it was very life-like but without color."

"Which one?'

"All of them, but especially the Apollo and Daphne. I can't get over the way the wind blew through her hair and the fabric of his robe flowed freely behind him, so alive; carved out of stone but as if they were breathing. It's like at any moment they'd break out of the marble and dance their way out of the museum. Did you read the story?"

"No."

"He pursued her relentlessly, you know. It's what Bernini portrays in the sculpture; Apollo chasing her, pleading and promising her everything. She begs with her father to make her ugly so that he'd stop hunting her, so her father transforms her skin into bark, her hair into leaves, and her arms to branches.

"That'll do it."

"Well, it didn't. Even in this form Apollo still loved her."

"Those who pursue fleeting forms of pleasure, in the end, find only bitter berries in their hands."

"You did read it!"

"Only the engraving."

She pushed at him playfully. Then she leaned over the rail and took in the fantastic view.

"If only it could last forever."

"Nothing does."

"Don't be so fatalistic."

Suddenly the woman looked down at her purse. She opened it and looked through it. "I left my perfume on the counter!" she cried out.

"What?"

"My perfume! I left it on the counter in the bathroom at the hotel. We have to go back!"

"What?"

"It's *Chanel*, they'll take it."

"I don't think so."

"Yes, its expensive stuff."

"It will be fine."

"You think?"

"Yes, I think so."

"But I'm worried about it."

"Don't be." He turned and leaned forward. "Let's enjoy the view."

There were many other tourists on the terrace, indulging in the view and taking photographs. Garrett looked at them, and as he did he thought about what the woman had said, about all the many people who had come and gone from this city. They are all ghosts, he thought, like the Bernini. Like the thousands of people who had roamed the streets of Rome in the past, these tourists will also be gone. Their time too will pass. So now he thought about it like he'd never thought of it before. It made him realize the fragility of the moment, and he suddenly felt overwhelmed by a sense of urgency. He looked around and saw an empty space at the balcony.

"Let's take a picture!" he said.

"What?"

"If you don't write it or photograph it, with time it never happened."

"What?" the woman asked.

Nearby a young German couple was standing at the balcony taking pictures. Garrett took the young woman's hand and led her over to them.

"Could you snap a picture for us?" he asked.

"Yes, of course," the young German man replied. "And maybe afterward you could do the same for us?"

"Sure."

Garrett pointed to the empty spot at the rail. "There?"

"Yes, of course," the German said.

Garrett handed the German his camera and led the woman over to the balcony.

"We have to go!" the woman said.

"This will only take a minute."

"I'm worried about my perfume."

"It will be okay."

They positioned themselves with their backs against the rail and the panorama of Rome behind them. The woman stood quietly as the German framed them in the shot.

"We are here together here in Rome," Garrett whispered softly. "Smile for the camera."

"Ready?" the German man asked.

Garrett pulled the woman close to him and wrapped his arm around her shoulder. The young woman forced out a smile, but she was still thinking about the bottle of *Chanel* sitting precariously on the bathroom counter.

The German centered the small digital screen and clicked the 'photo' button.

"Another?" the German man asked.

"Okay."

They repositioned themselves and the German snapped another picture. Then they swapped positions and Garrett took a few pictures of the German couple. Afterward, Garrett and the woman resumed their position at the edge of the terrace, leaning outwardly against the ancient marble balcony.

"Let's go," the young woman said.

"There's the Campo de Flori," Garrett said, pointing off into the distance.

"Where?"

"There!" he pointed again, more precisely. "That's the place we had dinner last night."

"That's it?"

"Yeah."

"Do you think your mother would like to return to Rome?" he asked.

"Of course she would. If only she could make the trip."

"It's possible, I think. Of course she'd need some assistance."

"Too bad there's not a cure for arthritis."

"Everything's curable except death."

The *Chanel* again weighed heavily in the young woman's mind and a mortified expression returned to her face. "Let's go!"

"Wait," Garrett replied, holding her arm back gently. "Look at it."

"What?"

"Look at it!"

Garrett could smell the aroma of cypress coming from the

tall, narrow trees growing along the side of the terrace. The dark green needles, warmed by the sun, gave off a scent of fresh cut pine. He breathed it in deeply through his nostrils and let the sun soak into his face.

"Let's go," she said.

He took her hand and together they rushed down the steps back to the Piazza del Popolo.

Randy Osborne

Warehouse

Judge John S. Flanders fixed me with hooded eyes. His hairy sausage fingers fumbled with the paperwork. Wet lips peeled away from yellow teeth.

I felt sick and dizzy.

"Who comes before us now?" Flanders boomed at me, drowning out my heart's thunder.

It was 1965. Lyndon Johnson sent the first troops to Vietnam that year. Malcolm X was shot to death. Race riots tore up the South. In my hometown of Rockford, Illinois, I walked with my cousin Patrick and his brother Mike into an open building from which I took nothing. Then we all got arrested.

In those days, the phrase "juvenile delinquent" carried weight. It meant leather jackets and smoking. Fast cars, vandalism, and getting girls in trouble. At age 10, still without pubic hair, I became a juvenile delinquent.

True, I was not a well-behaved boy. I loved the tick made by a stone as it passed through glass, leaving a jagged hole, followed by the festive tinkle of glass and the stone's muted clatter, ricocheting inside the garage. One night I broke more than 100 windows.

But "burglarized"—the word used by police for our (non-) caper—was inaccurate. At most, Patrick (my age), Mike (a few years older), and I *trespassed upon* Seipel & Sons Electrical Supply Warehouse. Most boys in the neighborhood did likewise. The ramshackle four-story building stood unguarded, its half-open door creaking loose. Some kids swiped switches, screws, bundles of multicolored wire, but I saw zilch that interested me. Nor did Patrick.

Mike started out small, taking flex cord, caddy clips, locks, and tape. He moved up to soldering irons, crimpers, glue guns and drills. Near the end, he walked out of Seipel with a suitcase-like object, later opened in his bedroom to reveal an array of plugs and dials. Tube tester, he said.

Boys from a rival bunch spotted us. More to the point, they spotted Mike, lugging the tube tester behind him like a kid on his way to the train station. They dropped the dime on Mike because they hated him. Mike: always ready to fight, always ready to squeal on *them*.

I heard about the cops' visit to his house from Patrick. "Like hell," Ted told the juvie badges when they showed up at his door. Father to Patrick, Mike and two more kids, Korean War veteran Ted wouldn't let officers inside without a warrant. Patrick hovered behind his dad, guessing the nature of the trouble and preparing to act confused. Mike already had fled.

"Who comes before us now?"

Today I understand Flanders' roaring routine as theatrics, as judicial Wizard of Ozzery thrown in to terrify his victims, because he could and enjoyed it.

In court, the sneering blowhard Flanders targeted Mike first, likely wanting to break the spirit of our ringleader, make an example of him so that his henchboys then would cave in and confess.

Mike shivered like a dog in the rain. His lanky frame twitched uncontrollably, as if zapped by some hidden device, maybe taken from a shelf at Seipel & Sons. "He's going to crap his pants," Patrick muttered beside me.

Patrick believed our court appearance amounted to nothing more than a formality to satisfy the grown-ups. We had, after all, done nothing wrong. I felt almost the same, about 75 percent certain that I would be shown mercy, if not exonerated altogether. *Exonerated* was my mother's word. I had disgraced the family, she said, as if we had been royalty or aristocrats to begin with. She wanted me "fully exonerated," our good name wiped clean.

Looking around, I noticed that my mother was one of the few adults not smiling along with the gruesome Flanders. Most of the parents seemed weirdly pleased by this theater of disgrace, and almost worshipful of Flanders, as if he would deliver at last an effective penalty, one that made their children fall into line, finally behave.

Ted, arms crossed, scowled at the judge.

I'd like to reel off the insults Flanders pelted Mike with, the shape of the humiliation Flanders wrapped around this boy like a shawl of spikes, but I don't recall most of what he said, since I was not in the crosshairs. Not yet.

Patrick went next, and Flanders dispatched him quickly. When it was over, Patrick turned from the bench, putting on his best somber face. He jammed his hands in his pockets. During the long walk back to his seat, Patrick tried a sequence of expressions, as if hoping to hit on the most abject one for spectators. The people had come for this, we knew.

Then it was my turn. I wasn't able to push out a reply regarding Flanders' "who-comes" question—he already knew the answer anyway, since it was typed on the complaint—before the judge spoke his own response. As if he had just tasted something vile, he spat all three of my names, first, middle and last.

How would I like, he asked, to be thrown in jail that afternoon? He had seen boys like me, plenty of boys, turn into society's waste. Human garbage, unfit for the company of decent, hardworking people. A disease that festered, a pox that ruined what good citizens wanted to make for themselves.

On and on he went. My eyes burned.

Of course, none of us went to jail. With a royal slam of his gavel, Flanders declared us juvenile delinquents and placed us on probation for 18 months. If we had no further scrapes with the law, charges would be dropped at the end of the period and erased from the official records. And that's what happened.

Widely revered by Rockford's citizenry in the mindless way of crowds—in the way of our audience that day—Flanders was just a silly gasbag in a black gown: a big person who, I suppose for unsavory reasons if they could ever be known, took pleasure in bullying the little. He confirmed what I sensed about life at the mercy of power, and what Ted already knew.

My mother and Ted shared a secret link. He gave her small gifts, such as the sapphire brooch he claimed to have designed himself. His lapidary hobby gave me the idea that Ted was trying to replace my gem-cutter dad in a small way, although Ted must have known he would scarcely gain by it. After the divorce, my father became a pariah, seldom seen. Maybe Ted hoped to live by proxy a different life, not the reality of a factory foreman with a houseful of kids but the hero and comforter of a single mother, his sister-in-law.

Cleaning out my mother's attic after her death, I found a loose-leaf binder from Ted's soldier days. In front are charts he composed and formulas on the velocity of bombs aimed rightly. There's a treatise called the "Generalization of the Theory of Relativity for Explanatory Purposes." In the back of the book are notes that deal not with military tactics but criminology. They are dense, lengthy, scrupulously detailed, and a little goofball-ish. Combat must not have kept him busy enough. "So-called tangible evidence is often useless," Ted wrote, on the matter of investigations. He thumbed his nose at what he called "the conventional superstition of implacable avenging nemesis," which I guessed to mean he disagreed with the idea that bad guys always get caught. Or even that the "bad" guys are correctly identified. I gave the book to Patrick.

My mother circulated petitions to shut down the Seipel warehouse, an eyesore and health hazard neglected by its owners. But somebody found a quicker way. On the night the place burned down, Patrick said, he found his father on a lawn chair in the backyard, staring at the sky's orange blush, listening to the sirens. Dreamily, as if they were music.

In his criminology notes Ted equated any well-plotted caper to a fine painting that bears "the artist's personality and genius, his alone." The cops could read no signature on the unsolved Seipel fire, our town's biggest in years, an inferno. Like hell, as Ted might say, if you believed in Hades or, for that matter, justice—of which there was none but the imperfect kind you made yourself. We didn't belong with Flanders, Ted knew. He understood it the way he understood Einstein, and how fast bombs fall, and where to pour the kerosene.

Alice Hoffman
Conjure

It was August, when the crickets sang slowly and the past lingered in bright pools of glorious light, even though it would soon be gone, the way summer was all but over, yet the heat was still on the rise. The weather had been extreme that month: days of drenching rain, sudden showers of hail, temperatures passing record highs. Local children whispered that an angel had fallen to earth in a thunderstorm. There were roving groups who swore they had found signs. Footprints in the grass, black feathers, a campfire in the woods behind the high school where there were sparks of shimmering ash. One neighborhood boy vowed that he had seen a man in a black cloak rise above the earth and walk on air, and although no one believed his account, mothers began to keep their children home. They locked the doors, called in the dogs, kept the lights on after dusk.

No one cut through the field anymore, except for Abbey and Cate, best friends, who at age sixteen were too old to be kept home and far too sure of themselves to be afraid of a story. They had jobs at the town pool as swim counselors, and late in the afternoons they walked home together, arms draped over each other's shoulders, making their way through the pale heat, their long hair scented with chlorine. Usually they stopped at the library, where Cate would wait outside, dreamy-eyed, while Abbey ran in to find a new book, which would get her through the night. She'd had trouble sleeping lately, and books were her antidote to the darkness of these late-August nights. She had the distinct impression that something was beginning and something was ending; there were just so many days like this left to them. Before they knew it, time would speed up and the future would appear on a street corner or in a park, and there they'd be, grown women who'd forgotten how long a summer could last.

The librarian, Mrs. Fanning, often had a stack of books waiting for Abbey, and choosing the right one had become a sacred ritual. On this day Abbey returned *Great Expectations* and took up Ray Bradbury's *Something Wicked This Way Comes*.

"Excellent choice," Mrs. Fanning said, pleased. "By the pricking of my thumb, something wicked this way comes. The title comes from *Macbeth*, Act IV."

"Do you believe people are wicked?" Abbey asked.

Outside the world was green, shifting in the dappled light. Cate was sitting on the steps, head thrown back, basking in the last of the sun. If Abbey tried to talk about her worries with her friend, Cate would admonish her. "You think too much!"

"Certainly some people are," Mrs. Fanning said." But there'd be no interesting novels without them, would there?"

In a fiction it was possible to discern the wicked from the pure of heart. Roses withered when devious individuals passed by; blackthorns grew about them. But such clues were not as evident in real life. "Judge a person the same way you judge a book," Mrs.

Fanning suggested. "A search for beauty and truth, a gut response to what feels a lie. Intuition." She seemed quite sure of herself. "Imagination."

Abbey began reading on the way home from the library, acting out all the parts. She concentrated so deeply on the words on the page that she stumbled over shifts in the concrete sidewalk.

"You live in books." Cate grinned.

"I would if I could," Abbey admitted.

"What's the good of that?" Cate sighed, for she yearned for real life. She wanted adventure, one-of-a-kind experiences. She was suddenly beautiful and there were teenage boys who followed her around town, just as suddenly in love with her, though they were still too young to say so. She confided that her plan was to leave town after high school graduation, find her way to California, see every bit of the coast. She'd study butterflies in Monterey, sharks in San Diego. She had a fearless nature, which was why Abbey both admired her and was concerned for her at the same time. They were nearly home, but Cate lagged behind, gazing over at the field, the one wild piece of land left in town.

"What would you do if you saw an angel?" she asked in a low voice.

They stood together on the corner, where they met every morning.

"There's no such thing," Abbey said. "Not around here."

"If there was." Cate squinted to see into the distance. "Seriously."

"I'd write about him," Abbey said.

As for Cate, they both knew she'd fly away, triumphant and distant in the arms of an angel.

* * *

It was Cate who insisted they take the shortcut the following afternoon, forsaking the library, so they might walk through the field where the angel was said to be.

"How many times do you get to search for an angel?" she teased, running off before Abbey could say that if there was such a thing, perhaps it wasn't meant to be a sight for human eyes, that the very brightness of such a creature might burn and blind anyone who gazed upon him. Cate had already climbed the fence that separated the path from the field, and Abbey had no choice but to follow, up and over the fence, leaping clumsily onto the ground. The books she'd meant to return to the library weighed down her backpack. Cate grinned and pointed to a dark splotch on the ground. It was only a single feather in the tall grass beside the creek, but when Cate ran to grab it, Abbey felt a hollow chill. The water in the creek was green, slow-moving, and swirls of insects rose from it. They used to swim here when they were younger, practicing the backstroke and the butterfly.

Cate ran back, her hair flying out behind her. She held up the feather. "We're definitely on the right path." She elbowed Abbey, then nodded to a willow tree. A young man in a black coat was gazing at them. Abbey took a step back. He was wearing leather gloves though the weather was fine.

"Don't tell me you're afraid?" Cate teased. "He's probably Bobby Marcus's cousin."

Bobby Marcus was their twelve-year-old neighbor who'd told everyone that his cousin from Los Angeles was spending a few weeks with them, and that he slept all day and was out all night. Not that there was anywhere to go in their town in the evenings, only the Blue Note Bar and Grill, where some of their fathers stopped on the way home from work.

Dusk was falling down among the trees. The swirls of insects above the creek turned blue in the murky air. The young man had long dark hair and an easy gait. He had dramatic features, gray, light-filled eyes. He looked a few years older than the girls, perhaps nineteen. He was making his way through the tall grass, approaching as if he knew them and was meant to speak to them, as if he'd been sent to them on this evening in August. Most people were now at home, sitting down to dinner, and Abbey's mother would be watching from the door. She worried about her daughter, who spent so much time alone. She'd be even more concerned if she knew that there were nights when Abbey climbed out her bedroom window so that she could amble through town in the dark. Abbey had never even told Cate that she climbed out her window on restless nights, her feet landing in the ivy. Sometimes she went to sit on the stone steps of the library, wondering about the world beyond their town; other times she came to this very field and read by moonlight, savoring her aloneness. Now she wasn't certain she'd come back here again. The edges of the grass were sullen and plumy in the shifting light.

Cate went forward. The young man in the black coat had clearly been drawn to her luminous beauty. He had a slow, winning smile, which he aimed at her. Abbey saw that his boots were covered with a layer of gray ash and that the fabric of his coat was frayed.

"I'll bet you're Bobby Marcus's cousin," Cate said as they approached each other. If Abbey didn't know any better, she'd think her friend was flirting.

"That's me." He said his name was Lowell. He grinned broadly when Abbey gazed at his gloves. "I've been chopping wood," he explained. "I've been camping here all summer. I can't bring myself to sleep under a roof."

Abbey had never seen him here on the nights when she'd come to read in the grass. She wondered if angels lied, or if that was only the territory of men.

Lowell offered them a drink. "I'm being sociable and you should be too. Whatever your parents say, you're old enough for a beer."

His invitation seemed more like a challenge. All the same they followed him through the grass to his campsite. "We're only being polite," Cate assured Abbey when she hesitated. "He's right—we're old enough."

There was a pot for boiling water, a sleeping bag, a small canvas tent, a small axe.

"For chopping wood," he said to Abbey, throwing down his gloves.

There was no stack of firewood, only some boughs from a twisted bramble tree. Abbey imagined he wasn't a practiced camper, that he was a city boy who couldn't even read a map of the stars. When Lowell reached out to get them some beers that he kept cooling in a fishing net in the creek, Abbey spied a black dog tattooed on his wrist. She felt a tightness in her throat, but she sipped at the cold beer, sharing a bottle with Cate. The girls sat close together on a log, and Abbey thought she could feel her friend's heart beating alongside her own. The more beer the girls drank, the more Lowell talked. He told them about California, how beautiful it was, how the sky stretched on forever, how the night smelled of gardenias. He was a handsome young man, with a graceful way of speaking, and by the time he was done, California seemed like the promised land, a heaven all its own.

"That's where I'm going," Cate said.

"I knew that was what you wanted." Lowell laughed. Abbey noticed that he seemed impressed by his own observations, the sort of man who had learned a lot about women in his lifetime and was quick to put these lessons to use. "I could see it in your future."

Cate laughed, flattered, lowering her eyes. She was demure in a way Abbey had never known her to be. "You don't even know me," she said to Lowell, as if she wanted him to.

"You don't believe me?" Lowell shifted over to sit beside Cate, his leg against hers. "I know you real well. I can see everything that's going to happen to you."

Abbey tugged on Cate's sleeve. The intuition Mrs. Fanning had referred to felt slick, as if oil was pooling around them, dark and unstoppable. This late in August, time was already shifting, the light disappearing before anyone expected it to. "We have to go," she urged.

"Keep me a secret," Lowell said. He leaned close to Cate when he spoke, his breath moving the strands of her hair. His gray eyes were half closed, as if he was in the middle of a dream and that dream included Cate and her future. "I'd hate to be chased out and forced to sleep under a roof."

Cate promised they would make up a story; they'd say they'd stayed late to practice their lifesaving techniques at the pool. In the darkening light, the ends of Cate's hair looked faintly green, tinted by chlorine; perhaps the lie she intended to tell had turned her hair this color, or perhaps it was only the fading of the day that made it seem so.

Lowell walked them to the edge of the field. Abbey went first because she knew where the briars were; Cate came next, with Lowell following. Right before they stopped out of the tall grass, Abbey turned to see him kiss her friend. By then, it was dark.

That night Abbey climbed out her window. She kept her shoes under the porch steps, but tonight she went barefoot. She made her way through town, as she always did. Usually the darkened houses brought her a sort of comfort, but tonight the silence rattled her;

she could feel it hitting against her bones. She stopped at the edge of the field. She thought she saw him beneath the tree, wearing his black coat and his gloves. She didn't see an angel but a man, waiting for something, twisting the future into rope of his own devising. Abbey had that same chilled feeling she'd had when she'd first spied him. She turned and ran, feeling the threat he cast until she reached her corner. She went past her own house and sneaked into the Marcuses' yard. She threw a pebble at the window. She threw another and another, and finally Bobby appeared.

He opened the window and leaned out, confused. "Are you crazy?" he whispered, waving his arms at her. "Go away."

"Where's your cousin?" Abbey wanted to know.

"He went back to California, " Bobby said. "My parents kicked him out."

He shut his window, not wanting to say more, but Abbey sat down at the Marcuses' picnic table to wait. After a while Bobby came out. He was only twelve, and Abbey had babysat for him once or twice, a fact he hated to be reminded of whenever she teased him, recalling how he used to cry to get his way. He was wearing a raincoat over his pajamas.

"Why'd they kick him out?" Abbey asked.

Bobby shrugged.

"There must have been a reason."

Bobby's parents were both teachers at the high school, warm-hearted, reasonable people.

"He was inappropriate," Bobby said.

Abbey felt that chill. "Meaning?"

When Bobby clammed up, Abbey grabbed his arm and twisted. She was stronger than she appeared, perhaps from carrying stacks of books home from the library.

"Hey!" Bobby pulled away. "Okay. Fine. He said he could see

the future."

"They kicked him out for that?"

"Well, they thought he was crazy. I mean he went on and on about it, like he was cursing us or something. He wasn't like that when he first came here. He sat with my mother for hours in the kitchen; he cut the lawn. Then he snapped and started saying he knew our fate and that we deserved everything we got."

Abbey recalled the way Lowell walked toward them, his gaze set on Cate.

"And I guess when they called California they found out he's been in a lot of trouble. He's not really even a cousin. He was just working for my uncle, and he stole his car. He took things from here, too," Bobby said, moody, clearly having been told to keep the family troubles private.

"What kind of things?"

"He made me promise not to tell."

Abbey grabbed Bobby's arm and he shifted away. "Stupid things. Rope. Packing tape. Blankets. He took my dad's axe that we used when we went camping."

"What did he tell you about the future? Are you going to be a millionaire?"

Abbey was sarcastic by nature; her mother often complained about this, as well as her having her head in the clouds. Her mother insisted that Abbey would be beautiful if she stopped chopping her hair short and paid some attention to her appearance instead of wearing shorts and T-shirts and old hooded sweatshirts.

"He told my dad he'd be dead by December," Bobby Marcus said.

"What does he know?" Abbey snorted. "He's not a doctor."

"My dad has leukemia." Bobby's voice was solemn. Abbey knew Mr. Marcus had been ill, but people in town didn't know just how sick he'd been, only that he was once stout and was now painfully thin. "He's been in remission."

Until this summer Abbey felt that nothing could touch the people close to her. Then she had started worrying, and once she'd started she found she couldn't stop. "Don't worry about any of Lowell's predictions. He seems like a big liar."

"I don't know." Bobby looked younger than his years. "My father didn't get out of bed today."

At the pool the next day, Cate kept to herself. A light rain started to fall in the afternoon, and when the swimmers scattered into the locker room Cate just sat there on the concrete, rain streaming down. She looked like a water nymph, a creature who belonged to another element.

"You're going to get soaked," Abbey called as she scrambled to find a dry place under the patio awning.

"It's only rain," Cate said, as if the world around her didn't matter, as if she was already in some other, unreachable place, a realm much farther away than California.

Once she was underneath the awning, Abby started reading and soon she was in another world herself. Then, all at once, she felt someone was drowning, even though there were no swimmers in the pool. When she looked up Cate was gone. There was that chill, right through her sweatshirt. She waited, anxious and ready to bolt, until all of the campers were picked up by their parents, then she took off running. The rain was coming down harder. She climbed the fence, snagging her fingers on the metal, then ran along the creek, now rushing with rising water. She imagined him gone; she willed it with all her might. But his tent was still in the field, and there were wisps of smoke from a bonfire that had been doused by the torrents. She went within feet of the tent and called, "Cate?" in a low, shaky tone, but there was no answer and she couldn't tell if anyone was in the tent, if what she heard was a girl's voice or only the sound of the rain.

The next morning Cate wasn't waiting on the corner where they usually met. There were several police cars circling the neighborhood. In a panic Abbey ran all the way to the pool. She had a dark premonition and was quick to berate herself for not warning Cate against Lowell. An angel, a liar, a man with black gloves. But there was Cate, calmly teaching the youngest swim group how to dog-paddle.

"Where were you?" Abbey said as she came up beside her. There was the thrum of panic in her throat as she spoke.

Cate kept her attention focused on the Guppies. "Kick," she called out to them before she turned to her friend. "We don't have to do everything together, do we? Anyway, you were the one who was late."

All that day Cate avoided her, but at their lunch break, Abbey made a point of sitting beside her at the picnic table. "He's not even Bobby Marcus's cousin."

Cate coolly appraised her as she continued eating her lunch. "I know." Her wet hair streamed down her back.

"And he's a thief," Abbey said.

Cate threw her a contemptuous look. "You think you're so smart."

"Were you with him when I came looking for you yesterday?" Abbey's voice sounded broken even to herself.

"He said you'd be jealous."

"You think I'm jealous? Abbey stood up, her heart hitting against her chest.

Cate shrugged. "You tell me."

"Did he tell you Bobby's father kicked him out? That he stole a car in California?"

"He told me everything," Cate said calmly. "He told me you can't be friends with someone who's filled with envy."

"Is that what he told you about the future? That we wouldn't be friends anymore?"

"He said I'd be leaving for California before I knew it."

Late in the afternoon Abbey told the head counselor that she felt ill and needed to go home. It wasn't exactly a lie. She packed up her swimsuit and her books and left early, her head throbbing. She walked to the field, then scaled the fence. She stood beside the creek. She wasn't surprised by what she saw. There was now a car parked under the bushes, hidden by briars and leaves. You had to squint to see it beyond the tree, then it was possible to make out the Marcuses' old station wagon, which Bobby's father had reported missing that morning. That was why there were police cars patrolling earlier in the day, looking for signs of a thief.

For a moment Abbey thought she might bolt and run, then keep on running till she had reached the far side of the field. Instead, she studied the stolen car, the briars, the field she had come to all her life. She thought about the items he'd taken from the Marcuses' garage—the tape, the ropes.

He was there, under the tree. He laughed when he saw her, and waved her over. He was graceful and tall and sure of himself. She walked through the high grass, and it stung when it hit against her legs.

"I knew you'd show up," he said when Abbey reached his campsite. "You and I made a connection. She thinks she's the one that everyone wants, but it's you. I can see what's beautiful about you." He cupped Abbey's chin and studied her face. She understood how he could make someone feel special.

Abbey saw then that he was older than they'd first thought, not seventeen or eighteen but in his mid-twenties. There were feathers around the campsite because he was trapping birds for his supper. There were the bones of sparrows and larks, white and stripped bare. She thought about the children who believed an angel had fallen into the field, convinced that a miracle would soon occur. She thought about the volumes in the library that were waiting for her on the shelves, each one beautiful, each one-of-a-kind.

He kissed her and she let him. Soon enough someone would notice the stolen car. He wouldn't keep himself hidden in this town; he'd have use for the ropes, the tape, the axe, all that he'd need to take someone with him tonight. Maybe he'd stop in a field far from here, in another town, where a girl's body wouldn't be identified; maybe he'd keep on driving. He kissed her and she kissed him back. She knew that Cate would follow her into the field, and that she'd spy them together, then turn and run, distraught.

When he grabbed Abbey to pull her toward the car, she slipped out of his grasp, leaving him holding on to nothing but her backpack full of books. She was wearing shorts and a sweatshirt and the sneakers her mother told her were unfashionable. She ran home as if she were the angel with black wings, and she didn't climb out her window again after that. In fact she kept it locked. She knew that Cate would cry all that night and that she'd never talk to Abbey again, just as she knew that years later, when Cate came home for a visit from California, compelled to stop at the library to confront her old friend, demanding to know how she could have betrayed her so easily, Abbey would simply tell her that the man in the field wasn't the only one who could see the future.

.

Contributing Authors

MORT CASTLE is a horror author and writing teacher who has published over 500 short stories. Twice a winner of the Black Quill Award and the Bram Stoker Award, Castle edited *On Writing Horror,* the primary reference work for writers of dark fiction. He lives near Chicago with Jane, his wife of 40 years.

WILLIAM FALO's stories have appeared or are forthcoming in *Emrys Journal, 34th Parallel, Skyline Review, Foliate Oak Review, Oak Bend Review, Open Wide Magazine, The Linnet's Wings, The View From Here, The Monarch Review*, and others. He was nominated for a Pushcart Prize.

ALICE HOFFMAN is the author of many bestselling novels including *Practical Magic, The Red Garden*, and *The Dovekeepers*. Hoffman's work has been published in more than twenty translations and more than one hundred foreign editions. Her novels have received mention as notable books of the year by The New York Times, Entertainment Weekly, The Los Angeles Times, Library Journal, and People Magazine. She has also worked as a screenwriter and is the author of the original screenplay "Independence Day" a film starring Kathleen Quinlan and Diane Wiest. Her short fiction and non-fiction have appeared in The New York Times, The Boston Globe Magazine, Kenyon Review, Redbook, Architectural Digest, Gourmet, Self, and other magazines. Her teen novel Aquamarine was recently made into a film starring Emma Roberts.

DENTON LOVING lives near the historic Cumberland Gap, Where Tennessee, Kentucky, and Virginia converge. He works at Lincoln Memorial University, where he co-directs the annual Mountain Heritage Literary Festival and serves as executive editor of Drafthorse: the literary journal of work and no work (www. drafthorsejournal.orge). He is also editor of Volume 4 of the Motif Anthology Series, published by Motes Books. His fiction, poetry, essays and reviews have appeared or are forthcoming in River Styx, [PANK], Main Street Rag and in numerous anthologies.

ERIC CHARLES MAY is an associate professor iin the Creative Writing department at Columbia College Chicago. A Chicago native and former reporter for the Washington Post, his fiction has appeared in the magazines *Fish Stories*, *F*, and *Criminal Class*. In addition to his *Post* reporting, his nonfiction has appeared in *Sport Literate*, the *Chicago Tribune*, and the personal essay anthology *Briefly Knocked Unconscious by a Low-Flying Duck*. His first novel, *Bedrock Faith*, was published in 2014 by Akashic Books.

MIKE McCORKLE is an emerging fiction writer and freelancer based out of Seattle. He recently spent a year living in Mexico instructing English and now works as a writing mentor and private instructor in the south Puget Sound. When he is not writing, Mike can found exploring the backwoods with his son Rylan and Labrador Betsy.

PATRICIA ANN McNAIR has lived 98 percent of her life in the Midwest. She is an Associate Professor in the Department of Creative Writing at Columbia College Chicago, where she received the Excellence in Teaching Award as well as a nominatin for the Carnegie Foundation's US Professor of the Year. McNair's story collection, *The Temple of Air*, was named Chicago Writers Association Book of the Year in traditional fiction, Devil's Kitchen Reader Awardee in Prose, and finalist in adult fiction by Society of Midland Authors. She's received numerous Illinois Arts Council Awards and Pushcart Prize nominations in fiction and nonfiction, and her work has been named a finalist for the American Fiction Prize twice.

CHRISTINA MURPHY'S stories have appeared in a range of journals and anthologies, including *A Cappella Zoo, [PANK], Word Riot, Spilling Ink Review*, and *The Last Word: A Collection of Fiction*. Her fiction has twice been nominated for a Pushcart Prize and was the winner of the 2011 Andre Dubus Award for Short Fiction.

SAHAR MUSTAFAH is a writer, editor, and teacher from Chicago. Her work has appeared in *Word Riot, Hair Trigger 35, Mizna, New Scriptor, Chicago Literati*, and *Dinarzad's Children: An Anthology of Contemporary Arab American Literature* (2004). Her short story "Shisha Love" won the 2012 Guild Literary Complex Fiction Award and was nominated for a 2013 Pushcart Prize; her short story "Perfect Genes" earned 3rd Place in the 2013 Gold Circle Awards from Columbia University Scholastic Press Association for collegiate magazines. She received her MFA in fiction writing from Columbia College Chicago and is the co-founder and editor of *Bird's Thumb*, a literary journal.

RANDY OSBORNE's work has appeared in small literary magazines. He teaches fiction and creative nonfiction for the continuing-education program at Emory University in Atlanta. He is finishing a book of personal essays, and is represented by Brandt & Hochman in New York. You can find more about his current work at www.randyosborne.com.

Z.E. RATCHES lives in Tigard, Oregon, which Z thinks is a really funny sounding name for a town. Z is the oldest (and shortest) of three children and grew up next door to George Washington in Mount Vernon, Verginia. Z graduated from Virginia Commonwealth University. Z also went to law school, but doesn't like to talk about it.

CYNTHIA SCOTT is a freelance writer, blogger, and copyeditor at Zharmae Publishing Press. Her fiction and essays have appeared in *Graze Magazine, Dogplotz.com, eFiction, Bleed.com, Rain Taxi, Bright Lights Film Journal, Strange Horizons, Creosote Journal*, and others.

FRANK SCOZZARI's fiction has previously appeared in various literary magazines, including *The Kenyon Review, Tampa Review, Pacific Review, The Nassau Review, Berkeley Fiction Review, Ellipsis*

Magazine, Minetta Review, Eleven Eleven, South Dakota Review, Roanoke Review, Reed Magazine, Hawai'i Pacific Review, and *The MacGuffin.* Writing awards include Winner of the National Writer's Association Short Story Contest and three Pushcart Prize nominations.

MARY SKOMERZA is a graduate of The Evergreen State College with an emphasis in creative writing. She currently contributes to examiner.com. She has been writing for as long as she can remember and has a passion for alternative fiction and the writers who have chosen to push the boundaries of the written word.

STAR SPIDER is a writer from Canada where she lives with her awesome husband Ben Badger. Star is in the process of seeking publication for her novels while she writes and frolics on the beach. Her work can be found in *Gone Lawn, Aperion Review, Klipspringer Magazine, Close to the Bone, Black Treacle, ExFic* and *Grim Corps.*

Acknowledgments

"Altenmoor, Where the Dogs Dance" by Mort Castle, first published in *Twilight Zone Magazine* Vol. 2, No. 10, 1982.

"Conjure" by Alice Hoffman, first published in *Shadow Show: All New Stories in Celebration of Ray Bradbury*, edited by Sam Weller and Mort Castle. William Morrow, 2012.

SUBSCRIBE TO

FLYLEAF

at **FLYLEAFJOURNAL.COM**

Subscriptions to *Flyleaf Journal* are only $21 for a year. That's 14 short stories, each accompanied with an exclusively designed cover illustration. Our stories are printed so that they can be read anywhere at anytime, making them portable, shareable, and collectible. We encourage our readers to pass the stories along to friends and family once they have finished reading them. Simply sign your name on the back in the Reader History Log and send it off.